DAD'S LITTLE BOOK OF WISDOM

★ ★ ★

Earn More, Achieve More, & Live a Good Life

MARK FENNELL

www.dadslittlebookofwisdom.com

This is a work of nonfiction. Some names, characters, and places have been changed.

Library of Congress Catalogue Number available upon request.

First Paperback Edition

10 9 8 7 6 5 4 3 2 1

Produced by Raab & Co. | www.Raabandco.com
Cover Design by Andrew Bell

ISBN 978-1-7352490-0-1

Dear Kids,

I remember clearly the days each of you entered the world. I'm proud of you. Your mom and I feel blessed to have been entrusted with you and your development. You are each unique in gifts, talents, and interests. From holding your hand as you took your first steps, to teaching you to read, to steadying your bike as you learned to ride, I've been fortunate to be a part of your life.

As you embark upon the next phase of your journey, you'll no longer be under our roof. While you will not physically be living with us, you will not be alone. While you'll follow your own path, this guide will be here to make the journey a bit easier. As you encounter certain new situations, you'll have this trusted guide's advice, from someone who loves and cares about you.

Not everything in these pages will apply to you, or perhaps you will simply not agree with some of the advice. Over the years, you may grow in your own wisdom beyond what I've captured here. That's good!

You'll experience many firsts: attending college, starting your career, leading people, making major purchases, managing your finances, investing, developing new relationships, and perhaps starting a family. Through this, your faith will be there to guide you.

Your mom and I tried to teach you by word and example. This guide exists to start your early professional years on the right track, and to minimize the hard lessons later in life. This has been an exciting project, and it's dedicated to you.

I love you,

Dad

"In this insightful book, Fennell presents a very thoughtful, detailed, heartfelt, and practical guide for any and all young professionals. The reader will be inspired. But more so, he or she is given concrete, real-world wisdom, and solutions to succeed at the highest levels!"
— *Ryan O'Neill, Founder of The Minnesota Real Estate Team, #1 in Minnesota for 14 years; pianist in The O'Neill Brothers, streamed more than 1 billion times*

"I often wonder whether I have given enough instruction to my three boys. Did they listen? Will they remember? Did I cover everything? As I give each of them a copy of this book, I will let them know that the well-thought-out advice and views mirror mine and will put them on a path to success. A path that will help them avoid common mistakes and, most importantly, become a better person!"
— *Tommy Manion, VP of Operations, Superior Plus Energy*

"As a dad of three adult daughters, we have been given a gift from Mark, as he shares 20 years of life experience in the form of a toolbox for success. It's a complete reference guide for both young children and adult children trying to find their way in life!"
— *Mark Coleman, Strategic Account Executive*

CONTENTS

INTRODUCTION

"Dad, what advice would you give to your 20-year-old self?" That was a question my 11-year-old daughter asked me, and the answer is this book.

What you hold in your hands has the power to save years of painful experiences as you set off toward your personal, career, and relationship goals. All this in exchange for a few hours of reading.

As a father, my deepest desire is to pass what I have learned down to my children. I feel that in my lifetime, specifically over the past two decades, I have come to understand many intricacies of life and business that once baffled me. In this book I hope to share that Wisdom with you to help you along your own journey.

How should we define Wisdom, anyway? There is a whole book dedicated to it in the Bible, and philosophers have pontificated since the dawn of civilization about what exactly makes someone wise. To me, Wisdom is more of a feeling than a personality trait. It's not just being smart, nor is it being infallible. Much like Love, the concept of Wisdom is deeply meaningful to humankind, but is both mired in complexity and also bafflingly straightforward. For me, Wisdom is simply the ability to discern the right course of action when faced with a choice.

It's my sincere hope that both my children and readers will be able to make better life choices after learning from my experiences and the lessons I have extracted.

As you'll see, I enjoy popular quotations from culture's most influential figures, and I use their insight as a jumping-off point for many topics and explorations. One quote that most inspired me to write this book is from Ben Franklin, who said, "If you would not be forgotten, as soon as you are dead and rotten, either write things worth reading, or do things worth the writing."

In this book, I have attempted to both "write things worth reading" and share my most valuable experiences "worth the writing." These pages contain both the wisdom I've picked up throughout my years and the best of the books and quotes I've read. I'll also share my own personal journey to best illustrate the practical nature of the advice.

By focusing on my own unique strengths, I've been able to achieve a number of life goals, which include qualifying and running in the Boston Marathon; reaching the Top 3 in sales for my division of a global Fortune 500 company; accumulating wealth in the top 10 percent of the country; and generating income in the top 1 percent of individuals in the United States. More importantly, I enjoy authentic and loving relationships with my wife, our three kids, my parents, my four siblings, their families, and several close friends. I sincerely believe there isn't anything particularly special about me and what I've accomplished. Even with different abilities, anyone can enjoy as full of a life as they choose.

There were certainly struggles along the way. Mine began shortly after the start of my career. I had difficulty getting and staying motivated. I just couldn't seem to consistently achieve the results the company expected of me. I wondered what was wrong with me. I felt like an impostor and there were many days when I wanted to stay in my car and hide.

Even during times when I was selling well and my professional career felt promising, I got out of balance in my personal life by overcommitting to volunteer activities and other outside interests. I was so focused on pleasing other people that I failed to understand the negative impact it had on my most important relationships with my wife and kids.

Once I felt so lost and lacking motivation that I broke down and got professional help for depression. While I'm very glad I did now, at the time I felt ashamed. Other than my wife, I didn't let anyone know I needed professional help.

I would oscillate in and out of these episodes for over a decade.

During this span I was almost fired three times for poor sales performance. I thought the answer was to work harder, but that was just a short-term fix. My performance would improve temporarily and then my angst would kick in again and the pattern would repeat. I didn't recognize that I was in the wrong role and had deeply embedded limiting beliefs from years of the world's conditioning.

Finally, my mindset shifted. I started doing a few things differently. This change led to attracting more and more of the right people and opportunities into my life. I went from feeling like I was on a downward spiral to an upward one.

Almost everyone experiences ups and downs, and I wrote this book to help people mitigate that inevitable roller-coaster ride. I want to share with you the little things that made a big difference in my life so that — wherever you are in your life — you can get onto an upward spiral.

I'll show you how to start with your desires and fan those flames into a burning passion to begin to make them come true. You'll then learn how to achieve more of what you want most in life as we take your desires and clarify your goals and plans around them to make them a reality.

Once you have your plans clearly laid out, we'll cover the three most vital resources to making them become a reality: your attitude, your time, and your money.

We'll discuss your attitude, your time management, your money management, your communication skills, your decision-making skills, your personal relationships, and your faith.

Your attitude and willingness to put in the work and persevere for the long term will be your personal engine that will move you forward toward your goals. I'll share with you some inspiration and motivation from the greatest minds in history, minds that, in one way or another, have fueled me and can do the same for you.

Time is your most valuable resource and how you manage it will determine your ability to realize your goals. I'll show you how to best use this precious resource to achieve both the productivity *and pleasure you desire.*

How you manage your money will either lead you to financial security or financial desperation. I implore you to learn money management now and then act *immediately*. Delay and you may set yourself up for years of financial stress. I'll show you a few simple financial disciplines that, if adopted early in life, can virtually *guarantee abundance*.

Along your career journey you will need to develop new areas of knowledge and skill to serve you in the professional world. I'll share how to communicate effectively to customers and colleagues, as well as how to speak in front of crowds, which will help you in any line of business, and any aspect of life.

As you continue in your professional career, you'll be asked to make more and more important decisions. We'll cover how to think through those decisions and determine a course of action you can move confidently forward with. I'll share a method for evaluating a situation when you're stuck, as well as a tool you can begin to use today to help you build confidence in making decisions.

Regardless of professional success, or financial wealth, it will ultimately feel hollow without having solid relationships with the people you care most about and those who care about you. I'll share what I've found to be vital in continuing to connect with family and friends to make the one life we have most enjoyable and fulfilling.

I believe that a relationship with God is vital for any successful life and all too often neglected in our secular world. Too many people are growing up broken and disheartened because what they were told would make them happy has not. More than any other wish I have for you, I wish to save you from this heartache. If God and your faith are at the center of your life, I believe you're building your life on a solid foundation and can handle any of the storms that life will throw at you.

Finally, armed with all this insight, I'll share with you how you can use your knowledge, abilities, and mindset to lead others. But before you can effectively lead others, you must learn to lead yourself. You'll do this through how you conduct your life and the habits you adopt. By leading yourself well, you will grow confidently during your lifetime.

This will attract many opportunities and people into your life who will look for you to lead them.

If you put enough of the ideas in this book into action in your own life, combined with your own unique strengths, I'm confident you will be able to earn more, achieve more, and live a good life.

1

START WITH YOUR DESIRE

"Whatever the mind can conceive and believe, it can achieve."

Napoleon Hill

For many of my early professional years, I struggled chasing goals that weren't really mine. I found myself working hard toward achievements. I was frustrated that I couldn't seem to reach most of my goals, and when I did, they weren't nearly as satisfying as I expected.

For this reason, it's important to identify your goals and understand why you have them.

What do you want to do? Design the latest video game? Entertain millions with an animated movie? Write a best-selling book? Start a podcast? Create architectural marvels that touch the sky? Travel the globe?

In this chapter, I'll teach you to use your imagination to discover your true desires.

Look all around you. Run your fingers over the chair you're sitting on. Look at the windows outside. Study the cars. Each of these was someone's dream. Everything man-made is created twice. First in the mind's eye and then in reality. In this way, we are all God-like because of our ability to create. It's a wonderful gift, let's use it well!

1.1 Be Yourself

It's okay to be unique. The world will initially resist you choosing to be different, but if you persist, it will celebrate your uniqueness. The key is to be unconcerned with whether or not the world celebrates you.

When I was 13 years old, I was not comfortable in my own skin. I just wanted to disappear. I felt a bit like a ghost. I felt like I didn't fit in, and I felt alone. I looked around and didn't see people who liked me, and I didn't like myself. Overall, it was my life's lowest and most difficult period.

We had just moved from Florida to Texas during the middle of seventh grade. I went from having a good friend group to starting all over. Unfortunately, this new start didn't go well. I had trouble making friends and tried to be like others to fit in. This took a toll on me. I wasn't motivated in any particular direction. I was just existing. I had gone from someone who excelled at math before the move to someone who made poor grades for just flat-out sloppiness. Things began to improve when I graduated to high school — a different environment served me well. I made progress again when I left to attend the University of Notre Dame.

After graduating, I slipped back into old patterns of seeking to be someone I was not. I tried to force myself to look and act the part of a successful salesperson. I desired to earn more and achieve more — but for the wrong reasons and in a job that was a less-than-ideal fit for me. I didn't realize that at the time. I felt like I was driving a car with one foot on the accelerator while another foot kept slamming on the brakes, letting up and then slamming it down again. I couldn't let people in to see that I was struggling. As a result of this misguided desire, I was almost fired from my company for poor performance.

Through faith, growth, and the influence of the right people at the right time, I was able to find my way to feeling more and more comfortable in my own skin.

What are your unique gifts and desires? Are you able to hone those gifts while remaining unconcerned with whether the world celebrates you or not? This is a difficult task. William James, an American philosopher and psychologist considered to be the "Father of American psychology," realized that "the deepest principle in human nature is the craving to be appreciated."

But this craving often pressures us into putting other people's happiness above our own. It's a good thing that bold pioneers such as Walt Disney have shown the rewarding path that uniqueness provides. He once wrote that "the more you are like yourself, the less you are like anyone else, which makes you unique." He also admonished us, as the saying goes, to never forget that "to the world you may just be one person, but to one person you may be the world."

You are valuable for just being you. No one can be the brother, sister, son, daughter, father, mother, husband, wife, or friend you are. To the marketplace, your value may be measured in terms of what the market will pay for your skills, abilities, or creations. However, as a child of God and as a person, your value is immeasurable!

So, if you're innately valuable, how should you gauge your success? As Marcus Aurelius stated in the second century AD, "The true worth of a man is to be measured in the objects he pursues." Do you pursue personal wealth, fame, creating a loving family, growing your faith community, or a new car? Your choice will reveal what you hold important.

What inspires you to do your best? Competition? Creating amazing experiences? Having possessions? Striving to improve? Whatever it is, check your internal moral compass, and if you feel it's right, then go for it! When you pursue your dreams, you will feel alive and inspire those around you to do the same. In this way, you can change the world!

1.2 Get to the Finish Line

Once you determine the achievements that are important to you, be careful whom you share them with. Oftentimes, people may not be rooting for you or supporting you, even if they love you. Fear can stop them from fully accepting your goals. Feelings of shame may grip you if you've repeatedly announced plans to others but have not yet had them come to fruition or — worse yet — haven't even started on them. Share with people who can assist you. Share with people who care about you and wish to see you succeed. And perhaps most importantly, share with people willing and likely to hold you accountable for making your dreams a reality. My wife, Dana, is such a person for me. When I dreamily would lay out my pie-in-the-sky vision of qualifying for and running the Boston Marathon, my wife helped hold me accountable. I was able to accomplish that goal because of her.

I REMEMber the *BUZZ! BUZZ! BUZZ!* of the clock as I groggily rolled over and slapped the alarm off. I looked at the time. "5:45 a.m. and it's a Saturday," I grumbled to myself. My mind quickly raced through alternate scenarios. *Instead of getting up and running with this group of people I've never met, I could sleep in and run the local 5k instead.* That seemed a lot more appealing at the time. It's funny how creative your mind can become when faced with a challenge.

I was in the midst of convincing myself to take the easy way out — resetting the alarm clock for a later time — when Dana rolled over and asked, "Mark, what do you think you are doing?"

"I, uh, was going to sleep in and just run the local 5k at 9 o'clock instead."

"If you don't get up and run with this group, then I don't want to ever hear you talk about your goal to run the Boston Marathon again."

Wow! There she said it. I realized right then that if I was ever going to achieve my life goal of running the Boston Marathon, I needed to take the first step — literally.

The Saturday previous, I had run in the local Oak Ridge Elementary 5k. I was not in very good shape. I started from scratch and ran for two weeks beforehand to prepare. At this point I was barely able to run the 3.1 miles it would take to finish. In fact, in the home stretch, I was passed by a guy pushing his one-year-old daughter in a stroller! At the conclusion of the race, I went up to the person who finished second and was wearing a neon yellow racing shirt.

"Congratulations on your finish," I told him. "You ran very well."

"Thanks, I'm still recovering from running the Boston Marathon last week, but this was still pretty good."

"Wow! You ran the Boston Marathon! That's one of my life goals." I reached my hand out to shake his. "By the way, my name is Mark."

"Nice to meet you. Wayne. I run with a group called the Big 4 that meets every Saturday morning. You're welcome to join us if you'd like."

I was so excited when I first told my wife about that conversation. Now, at 5:45 a.m., my excitement seemed to have evaporated. I was trying to take the easy way out. Faced with the sobering decision between *easy* and what I *truly* wanted to do, I chose to take the necessary action. I got out of bed and showed up at the meeting spot.

Initially, the desire to enter into an elite group of runners got me excited. The Boston Marathon is the only marathon in the world that requires an individual to run another marathon fast enough to qualify. This was a massive goal, and it followed the advice of architect Daniel Hudson Burnham, "Make no little plans; they have no magic to stir men's blood [...] Make big plans; aim high in hope and work."

As I began to run with the group, I asked them questions. The more I learned, the more believable and realistic the goal of running the three hours and ten minutes for the full 26.2 miles appeared. This would require a pace of seven minutes and fifteen seconds a mile. I could easily run a single mile this fast, but could I sustain it for 26 miles? I had to if I wanted to achieve my goal. As author and leadership expert John Maxwell stated, "If there is hope in the future, there is power in the present." I had hope.

If you have a strong enough *why*, you can figure out any *how*. Your *why* will provide you the fuel and motivation. In my case, visualizing crossing the finish line for my qualifying race filled me with a sense of pride and excitement. I desperately wanted to tell people that I had done it. Since I had shared my desire with Dana, she encouraged me to act. From there, it was up to me to follow through.

So, how about you? What are you setting your sights on? Is your goal exciting enough to provide you power and energy each day? As the great Michelangelo once said, "The greater danger for most of us is not that our aim is too high and we miss it, but that it is too low and we reach it."

For your profession, remember that it's not just what you *get*, but what you can *give* or *grow through*. Don't choose to do the minimum. Instead, choose the most you can give. You'll find that your capabilities expand when you do.

The reasons for your desire need not make sense or appeal to anybody else, just to you.

1.3 Use a Magic Book

When my kids were young, I used to teach them the concept of desire and creation through the use of a Magic Book. The Magic Book was simply a few pages in my journal that would enable my kids to dream with their eyes open. That is, they could see their dreams written in front of them, and choose to make them a reality. We used the Magic Book to make board games, school projects, and pinewood derby cars. Occasionally, I would even bring it out when they wanted something — like a Captain America figurine or a Dora the Explorer backpack — to help them focus on a few items rather than everything in the store. We would follow three simple instructions:

1) Desire and Visualization: Close your eyes and picture it in your mind.
2) Specific Plans for Accomplishing: Write it down or draw it.
3) Take Action: Make it happen!

T.E. Lawrence, also known as Lawrence of Arabia, led an invasion during the First World War that others thought was impossible.

He stated,

> All men dream: but not equally. Those who dream by night in the dusty recesses of their minds wake in the day to find that it was vanity: but the dreamers of the day are dangerous men, for they may act their dream with open eyes, to make it possible.

If a little dreaming is dangerous, the cure for it is not to dream less but to dream more, to dream all the time. So, dream away! And dream with your eyes wide open and a pen in your hand!

1.4 Read Inspiring Books

When I was about to head off for college, I went to a garage sale with my mom. I came across a very old and tattered edition of Dale Carnegie's *How to Win Friends and Influence People*. I was amused as I recalled my dad's more modern version at home. While I waited for my mom to finish shopping, I began reading the introduction. It immediately captured my attention with the stories of how Carnegie had witnessed and explored the transformation of timid creatures into confident, successful, and fulfilled people.

This became one of the books that had the most influence on me. While there are many books that have impacted me, below are three that influenced me early in life.

1) *How to Win Friends and Influence People* by Dale Carnegie

I read it prior to attending the University of Notre Dame. I deliberately practiced the habits described in the book by learning names and introducing people to each other. Whereas in high school I was known to be more private and studious, in college I quickly developed a vast network of friends. This eventually led me to being elected co-president of my residence hall of about 300 people. Later, I was elected co-president of the Hall Presidents Council. One tip I learned from Carnegie's book was to make an effort to introduce people to one another to increase my friend network — and theirs. I would go out of my way to introduce students in different dorms to one another, especially when one was male and one was female. I did this and found myself suddenly popular!

2) *Think and Grow Rich* by Napoleon Hill

In 1908, young newspaper writer Napoleon Hill had the opportunity to interview steel baron Andrew Carnegie, one of the richest men of that time. Carnegie commissioned Hill to interview the most successful people of his era and distill their thoughts down into a philosophy to make their wisdom available to the masses. After investing 20 years of his life, the result was one of the best-selling books of all time, *Think and Grow Rich*.

I read this my junior year of college, following my first summer selling Cutco knives. This opened my eyes to a career in sales. It created a significant desire in me to be unique and able to make things happen. After reading this book, I knew sales would be a part of my life path.

3) *The Instant Millionaire* by Mark Fisher

This book taught me the concept of doubling your assets every year in order to become a millionaire. In the early years, this was easy. In later years, I wasn't able to maintain that pace, but it did get me started. The key was having a financial goal in mind. Having a target brings desire, energy, creativity, and the discipline to say no in the short run in exchange for a long-term success.

Years later, I would learn better approaches, relying on my character rather than any specific technique, but these books got me thinking and taking action. Books also helped unleash my imagination as to what was possible. For example, in reading *The Alchemist*, I was introduced to the concept of having a "Personal Legend" to strive to uncover and live out. This starts with listening to that small inner voice. For years, mine said to write a book and share my wisdom with the world. What is your inner voice calling you to do? Try listening.

1.5 Find Your Secret Motivation

While I'm not a particularly passionate basketball fan, I do love learning about the mindset and discipline that enables great sports figures to achieve their success.

For example, after LeBron James brought Cleveland its first major sports championship in 52 years, a reporter asked him, "What was your secret motivation?" James just smiled and shook his head. Since the beginning of the 2015 season, James had been hinting that he was driven by a secret motivation. While there was speculation that it was competition, considering many felt Steph Curry was a better player, it turns out it was a different motivator — being doubted. When James decided to move from Miami to Cleveland, some of his closest advisers and confidants told him he was making the biggest mistake of his life. That right there was his motivation. He was fueled by an inner desire to prove a specific doubter and naysayer wrong.

In my life, I recall an incident where I was likewise fueled by an inner drive to prove someone wrong. I had great respect and admiration for a colleague's technical knowledge and business acumen. However, she had been unsuccessful in achieving the results that she and the company had expected. The result was her leaving the company. I sought her out immediately upon hearing of her upcoming departure. She said to me, "Mark, you're never going to be successful in sales in this industry. You should go to work for a nonprofit." Looking back, perhaps she said it because she felt hurt, but at the time those words stung.

My confidence was shaken for months. Finally, I awoke to the reality that I could choose to believe her, or I could choose to take action and prove her wrong. I chose the latter. My desire wasn't about proving my success to her, it was about proving to myself that, "Yes, I could."

1.6 Dream the Impossible Dream

Competitive running has been around for over two thousand years. Throughout that time, it was generally believed to be impossible to run a mile in four minutes or less. Over the years, various doctors and scientists even offered their professional opinions and "medical facts" about how it simply wasn't possible for a human to accomplish such a feat. They bolstered their assertions by claiming that a human heart simply couldn't handle that amount of stress or wasn't physically able to manage that much oxygen.

Then, in 1954, to the astonishment of the running world, a runner named Roger Bannister came along and broke the four-minute barrier with a time of 3:59:4! And guess what? It didn't kill him. Once Bannister showed it could be done, others had no choice but to believe. Six weeks later another runner broke Bannister's record! Today, the one-mile record has dropped all the way down to 3:43:13. The only difference is belief!

Henry Ford is said to have come up with this masterful aphorism: "Whether you believe you can or whether you believe you can't, either way you are right."

You'll always have naysayers. They may even be people you respect and admire. However, impossible simply means it hasn't yet been done.

Keep in mind that your own resolution to succeed is more important than anything else. What is your desire? If you know what you want and want it badly enough, you'll find a way to get it.

1.7 Learn from My National Championship Story

Unfortunately, my former colleague's doomsday prediction had merit. At the time, I struggled with my own self-worth and ability to make decisions. How bad was it? I nervously fidgeted for an hour in a Target electronics aisle trying to decide if I should spend the $399 to buy myself an iPad. This seemed like such a large sum to be splurging on myself. I couldn't shake that feeling of apprehension and doubting voice in my head: "Mark, why should you be spending so much on yourself? That's selfish."

Fortunately, my boss had agreed to hire a sales coach to help me improve my sales performance. He assigned me an exercise entitled "Thoughts Are Things." First, I was to write down what was already in my life that I was grateful for. Second, I was to write down what it was that I desired to attract more of into my life. I then needed to read out loud my affirmation while looking into a mirror three times — upon waking, at lunchtime, and at night before going to sleep.

On Saturday, December 1, 2012, one of the affirmation statements I wrote down read, "I am thankful for a stream of memorable unique life experiences like attending the Notre Dame National Championship game in Miami."

Notre Dame's football team had just earned the right to play for the National Championship in January. Years earlier I had written in a journal that a life goal of mine was to watch my alma mater win the National Championship. The problem was, I didn't have tickets, transportation, or a place to stay. Attending would require all of these things and likely be prohibitively expensive. I felt it would be selfish of me to spend the money on me having this experience. Now my sales coach was encouraging me to affirm what I wanted from life.

Did it work?

I'll include the full unedited journal entry and let you decide.

Monday 12/3/12 @ 8:06 a.m.

Saturday morning I did the Sandler exercise of "Thoughts Are Things." I had to write down what I wanted to attract into my life. I wrote down, "... attending the Notre Dame National Championship Game in Miami on Jan 7th." My skepticism didn't want me to write it, I couldn't see how it was possible ... $1,400/Tix, plus airfare, plus hotel, rental car, parking, etc ... but I wrote it anyway! I wanted to have FAITH.

I said the affirmation twice that day before Mass. At Mass my mind drifted.

I thought if I could find a way to go, this could be a BREAKTHROUGH for me and my thinking. To break my self-limiting beliefs about something I desire costing too much, or me not being worthy. I thought about how there will be 80,000 in that stadium and I just wanted to be one of them. I thought about if I knew someone and they wanted me there, then my limitations wouldn't matter. I thought, "If only ... this would be the beginning of a new attitude. People who will be at this game are Winners. I am moving up, if only in my own self-esteem for being in that class of individual who knows what they want and makes it happen! If only I could find a way!" I was talking to God. I was praying. My FAITH may have been the size of a mustard seed.

Yet after Church we left, and I spotted Jim & Sarah I called out to them to celebrate the season. It turns out she was going and had an extra ticket. Had I not stopped to get out money to give to the Hurricane Sandy relief I may have never bumped into them!

IT IS ALL GOD'S PLAN!

My simple mindset change combined with taking action (and a little bit of luck) led me to have a once-in-a-lifetime experience. The costs were significantly less than I expected. I had a fantastic time in Miami with friends, met former Notre Dame stars Tim Brown and Brady Quinn, and even hung out on a yacht. It was an absolutely wonderful experience — except for the three hours of the game during which Notre Dame was crushed by Alabama 42–14. Ouch! While I couldn't control the outcome of the game, the realization that my change in thinking led to the experience happening confirmed for me that our belief *can* create our reality!

It wasn't long after I returned that my new belief in myself and my worth would come in handy in reshaping my destiny. As author Orison Swett Marden said, "Our destiny changes with our thoughts; we shall become what we wish to become, do what we wish to do, when our habitual thoughts correspond with our desires." My small investment in entertainment reaped a much bigger reward in my self-worth. Ultimately, this increased self-worth led me to taking a few bolder actions, which resulted in career and financial rewards for me and my family.

1.8 Instructions — Think on Paper

Once you've decided what you want to make happen, write it down. Make lists and prioritize your lists. This has the following three benefits:

1) Desires Become Real

In *Think and Grow Rich*, Napoleon Hill advises, "Reduce your plans to writing. The moment you complete this, you will have definitely given concrete form to the intangible desire." Put your clearly defined goal on paper. It will help galvanize the rest of you. This makes your desire tangible and believable.

2) Makes a Commitment

You may have lots of ideas that flitter into and out of your head. Consciously select one. Write it down. This will give it power.

3) Clarifies Your Thoughts

One method to clarify your goals is to ask "Why?" six times in a row. Ask yourself, "Why do I desire this?" Write down your answer, and then ask again about the answer. Keep going until you discover your true motivation, which may be levels below the surface. By uncovering it, you will understand the *real* reason you wish to accomplish a desire.

I have found when I am stressed or confused, this is one of the best steps I can take. It doesn't cost anything. It only takes a few minutes. The process of writing and then reading what you wrote will help unlock your mental inertia. I'll share more on affirmations in the next chapter.

1.9 Decide to Believe

After you decide specifically what you want, the next important step is to believe you can do it. Once again, William James weighs in: "In any project, the most important factor is your *belief*. Without *belief* there can be no successful outcome. My experience has been that your belief will create the actual fact. These are 'self-fulfilling prophecies.'" I 100 percent agree!

On the University of Notre Dame's campus there aren't fraternities or sororities, but the residence halls are all single-sex and serve as a place of friendship and identification.

As a freshman I was assigned to live in Keenan Hall. My enthusiasm was sky-high for my new home and what we could do there together, yet it wasn't matched by my dorm's upperclassmen. I felt deflated like a balloon letting out air when I noticed all the guys didn't share my excitement. A few made me feel like we were living in the worst dorm on campus. With the principles from *How to Win Friends and Influence People* still fresh in my mind, I secretly vowed to do something about it when I was in position to do so.

Later, as a sophomore, I found a kindred spirit who also wanted to improve the quality of life in our on-campus residence. We ran for and were elected co-presidents of Keenan Hall. The two of us decided upon our strategy to set the culture we wanted to promote and then introduce ourselves to the incoming freshmen. To win their hearts and minds, we decided first to focus on the fastest path to gaining their attention.

For incoming males, the number one thing they cared about was meeting females. We told them they were lucky to have been selected to live in Keenan as we had lots of activities that drew women in so they'd be able to meet them. We also told them that they'd have an opportunity to do their part. We brainstormed ideas and by setting the vision, these freshmen embraced it. Our assistant rector had the idea of doing a Halloween pumpkin-carving contest. We gave the freshmen leadership opportunities. They also created '70s night and '80s night parties. We hung giant posters in the female dorms advertising "Keenan Thursday Movie Nights," when movies were played in our basement common area. It worked! Our dorm generated more and more attention. The freshmen were excited about the role they were playing and felt lucky to be a part of it. The upperclassmen noticed all the activity and eventually came around. And it all started with a *belief* in who we were followed by *action*!

At the end of the school year, out of approximately thirty dorms, Keenan was recognized officially as "Residence Hall of the Year." It was nice, but seeing the enthusiasm, excitement, and brotherhood permeating our home was the real reward.

As Napoleon Hill says, "There is one quality which one must possess to win, and that is definiteness of purpose, the knowledge of what one wants, and a burning desire to possess it." We'll discuss goals and creating a vision later. For now, remember that if the picture of what you want is clear enough, it can fuel your belief to become a reality. The key to making things happen is painting a clear enough vision. Do so and others will follow you. *It is important to be clear in your own mind first!*

★ ★ ★

Some people have thousands of reasons why they cannot do what they want to, when all they need is one reason why they can. After you settle on what you truly desire, believe in yourself and get to work! If you don't know where to start, that's okay, we'll cover goal setting, goal planning, and goal achieving in the next chapter.

Take Action

- ☐ Write down your desires.
- ☐ Make sure they are *your* desires and not someone else's. Ask yourself, "Why do I want this?" Keep asking until you are six levels deep. Here you will find clarity about your true desires.
- ☐ Begin the habit of reading inspiring books. Start with the books listed at the end of each chapter.

Read These Books:

- ☐ *Think and Grow Rich* by Napoleon Hill
- ☐ *The Magic of Thinking Big* by David J. Schwartz
- ☐ *The Instant Millionaire* by Mark Fisher

2

CLARIFY YOUR GOAL

"When you want something, all the universe conspires in helping you to achieve it."

Paulo Coelho, *The Alchemist*

In his book *Explosion Green: One Man's Journey to Green the World's Largest Industry,* David Gottfried shares the story of how he was introduced to environmentally friendly construction. He explains that after returning home from the American Institute of Architects' annual conference in Boston, he found himself unable to sleep. He couldn't stop thinking about implementing green construction on a global scale. At that moment he decided, "This is what I wanted to do with my life."

Gottfried went on to create the U.S. Green Building Council, then the World Green Building Council, and the LEED rating system for buildings. His work has affected and improved construction practices around the world! And it all started with the clarity of his idea and his passion.

What is your problem or goal? Where are you setting your sights? Don't aim too low.

As entrepreneur and motivational speaker Jim Rohn says, "If you don't design your own life plan, chances are you'll fall into someone else's plan. And guess what they have planned for you? Not much!" It's true. No one cares more about your life than you. You need to take charge by deciding what you'll do with it. If you don't, you'll be at the mercy of others who may not have your best interests at heart. Author and personal development guru Brian Tracy agrees: "Those who do not have goals are doomed forever to work for those who do."

Set a goal big enough that in the process of achieving it, you become someone worth becoming. While you can certainly set goals for what you want to *get*, set goals for what you want to *become*.

Six years ago, I set an income goal that initially seemed outrageous as I wrote it. It was an exercise in belief. I've reached it, and now need to set a bigger, larger goal to help me stretch further. I realized along the way that the greatest benefit of this goal was not the money; it is in what I am becoming, and how I'm empowered to serve God.

Success is the progressive realization of a worthy ideal. The major reason for setting a goal is not for achieving it, but for what it makes of you to accomplish. It's in the striving that we are becoming the best version of ourselves.

Shortly after graduating from college, I came across the book *Instant Millionaire* by Mark Fisher. The concept of becoming a millionaire struck me. I set a goal to become a millionaire. I wrote down targets of what my assets and net worth would be by every birthday. While I did not reach every achievement by the date I originally targeted, I kept striving.

Over a decade later I met someone and we began reading and discussing *Think and Grow Rich* together. While I had read the book before, this time was different. My conversations with my new friend stretched what I believed was possible. This is what I wrote in my journal:

"I am realizing I have self-limiting beliefs holding me back. I set my sights too low on what I believe is possible for me. ____ earned $300k+/year for many years. I can do this too!"

While I could hardly fathom earning this much, in June 2014 I set earning $300,000 as my income goal. I created a statement of desire and worked toward it. It didn't happen by my original deadline, but I kept striving.

2.1 Instructions — Create a Goal

I've experienced both achieving goals as well as failing to achieve the goals I've set. I've also read significantly on the subject of goal setting and happen to be a big fan. I'll share a few of the things I've learned:

1) Assess Your Desire
2) Use the SMART System
3) Manage Your Beliefs
4) Focus Attention on a Few Goals

One of my first life goals was to finish a marathon. I did. However, since I didn't specify a target time it's no surprise that I didn't finish in a very fast time. I walked several miles and completed the race in five hours. After I successfully finished, my confidence and belief in myself grew — and so did my goal. I set my sight on running the Boston Marathon. For this I would need to run much faster. I had to finish another marathon in a time of three hours and ten minutes in order for someone my age and sex to qualify for the Boston Marathon.

To train, I ran twenty miles a week. This increased to regularly running thirty to forty miles a week. At the end, I ran over fifty miles a week to reach my peak running condition. It worked! This dedication and training enabled me to achieve my goal by running a qualifying time of 3:07, a dramatic reduction from my five-hour first marathon!

I'll illustrate how to implement the steps above on a goal by using my marathon goal as an example.

1) Assess Your Desire

Just wanting something is of little compelling force. Your level of desire must be greater than the difficulty and discipline required to achieve it. I had a burning desire to run a marathon and then to qualify for and run the Boston Marathon. There was no waffling. I was committed to making it a reality. You need to literally write down your goal.

2) Use the SMART System

The acronym SMART represents a way to set goals. It stands for:

Specific
Measurable
Achievable
Realistic
Time-bound

Below is an example applying the SMART System to my goal to run the Boston Marathon.

Specific: "I will qualify for the Boston Marathon by running another marathon in under 3:10."

Measurable: I could look at the stopwatch and know if I was successful or not.

Achievable: I looked around me and saw others who had achieved what I desired. I initially read Hal Higdon's *Marathon: The Ultimate Training Guide.* To qualify, I ran with a group of twenty guys and fifteen of them had run the Boston Marathon. I learned tremendously from them. This bolstered my belief that this was an achievable goal.

Realistic: I ran a few marathons prior to my qualifying one. Based on my times and physical condition, I felt I could achieve my qualifying time in a realistic time frame (less than a year of training).

Time-bound: I signed up for the Philadelphia Marathon, the completion of which would allow me to qualify for the Boston Marathon. All of my training was built around that date.

3) Manage Your Beliefs
Desire and belief are equally important in achieving a goal. Thanks to the advice from my mentors and through disciplined effort, my confidence grew to the point where I believed I could do it.

4) Focus Attention on a Few Goals
Limit your number of goals in order to keep them meaningful. Time is the most precious resource that we all have. When you select a goal, the most critical question you face is "How much time and effort are you willing to invest to achieve your desired outcome?" Saying yes to a desired

goal means also saying no to many other good and/or easier options. Most people aren't willing to commit wholeheartedly to one goal because it requires them to say no to the lure of the fun and easy in the short term. This is why so many people fail to achieve their stated goals.

I certainly fell into this trap of too many goals. I wanted to be a top salesperson, be promoted, acquire real estate, participate in a network marketing company, and begin a marriage — all at the same time! No doubt I frustrated my new bride. I failed in all but one of those goals, but at least I succeeded in remaining married!

2.2 Act Courageously

We are free to choose our path in life. We are faced with the choice to suffer one of two things: the pain of discipline or the pain of regret. While the pain of discipline weighs ounces, the pain of regret weighs tons. The pain of discipline will be quickly forgotten, while the pain of regret will be a weight around your neck that begins with the phrase, "If I only I would have …" So, while you may take action and not receive the outcome you intended, learn from it. Don't fear having the courage to act.

Once you set a goal, never let it leave your sight without taking action. This counts even for small goals. For example, if you have a goal to read a book, plan out when you will complete it. Write down your plan for reading certain chapters or pages by specific dates. If you wish to accumulate savings, take the first step of opening a savings account and transferring your first $100. Lao Tzu had it right when he said, "A journey of 1,000 miles begins with a single step." Just take action!

2.3 Don't Tell the World. Show It

Have you ever felt tempted to tell people about your lofty plans? That's normal, but not always helpful. Sometimes it's easy to get so caught up in describing what we're *going* to do that we never take any action. This was the trap I often found myself in early in my professional career. I would present in stunning detail all my elaborate plans to crush my sales goals. Managers would nod approvingly, and I felt good. I would tell a friend how

I was going to start a company. They would compliment me, and I would feel good. I would tell another friend about a magnificent real estate empire that I would someday oversee. I would crave and receive my friends' praise. But those good feelings were short-lived. I did a lot of *talking* and not much actual *doing*. This is not a good recipe, and I found out I was not alone in doing this. Be judicious about who you share your goals with and why; tell only a trusted few who will help keep you accountable.

In his book *Drive*, Daniel Pink describes how visualizations release endorphins similar to what we receive when we take action. It's this pent-up energy that provides the drive to persevere and make our dreams become a reality. Unfortunately, I was giving myself the reward — praise and a feeling of accomplishment — without doing the work and actually accomplishing anything. I was giving myself dessert before dinner and spoiling my appetite.

Now, when I'm about to start a new goal, I often have to remind myself to keep my mouth shut. I've had to tell a friend, "If I told you what I was going to do, I'd be way less likely to do it." How might adopting the motto "Don't tell the world. Show it" affect your life? Perhaps it's worth a try.

Have you felt the comfort of inaction? Of course! We all have. The reason is simple really: If you don't try, you can't fail. If you don't ask, you'll never be rejected — but you'll also never receive. A ship is always safest at the shore, but that's not what it's built for. It's built to go into the sea and the deep waters. Sure, it's risky, but the exciting new lands are on the other side.

2.4 Make Yourself Known

In my journal, I have a list of goals I would like to accomplish. One such item on my list was "Be involved in the making of a movie." In January 2015, my wife, knowing my goal, called me over after seeing a post on Facebook. "Mark, they're looking for extras in the next *Rocky* movie. Would you want to do it?" Would I want to do it? Of course! Since I knew what I wanted and let that desire be known by my wife, she was able to bring the opportunity to my attention.

On Wednesday, February 18, at 8:54 p.m., I received the email inviting me to be an extra for a "major scene that would involve multiple days of filming, starting on the 24th. Are you available?" I quickly responded, "YES!"

At 5:00 a.m., Tuesday, February 24, I woke so I could be at the designated shooting location by 6:00 a.m. When I arrived, there were already hundreds of people dressed in all sorts of styles.

While there, I met unemployed people, lawyers, social workers, company founders, independent filmmakers, and professional extras. It was quite a thrill to hear all their stories!

Since the notice I had received said to show up and essentially "be a fan in the crowd," I complied. I was grateful for my opportunity. I didn't care how big or small the role. As a result, I got a small role, which the director affectionately called, "background."

John, one of my fellow 1,100 extras who showed up that day, had a different plan. He received the same instructions, but instead of showing up as a fan, he dressed in a suit and tie. He looked important — too important to just be a fan.

He was an independent filmmaker and cinematographer. And he wanted a bigger role in the movie because it could lead to better things for him.

He went and hung out near the casting directors, telling me, "Nobody notices you when you're sitting down." Sure enough, his plan paid off. A casting director noticed him and asked him, "What's your role?" "I'm a fan," he replied. The casting director shook her head and said, "Not anymore. You've just been upgraded."

Because he chose to dress up and make himself known, John was cast as one of only three extras to be placed in the boxing ring. This guaranteed that he would be in the movie! I was happy for him as it was no doubt beneficial to his career. There were 1,099 other extras who could have done what he did. But only John took action.

2.5 Set Goals in Different Areas

What life dreams will you pursue this year? What lights your fire of desire and fuels you with the energy to pursue your passion? What are you saying to yourself?

"I will write a book!"
"I will become a millionaire!"
"I will run a marathon!"

These are dreams that you might say to yourself in that small quiet inner voice. But how do you take your hopes, dreams, and life desires and turn them into reality?

The indispensable first step to getting what you want out of life is to decide what you want. We have all been given the amazing and wonderful gift of being able to see into the future. As management expert Peter Drucker said, "The best way to predict the future is to create it." This applies in every area of life.

Even the great physicist Albert Einstein believed, "Imagination is more important than knowledge." Why did he believe this? Because knowledge is based on what is known, but imagination requires conjuring up novel and creative ideas. God the Creator made us in His own image, and when we create, we are embracing our birthright.

Let your imagination run wild. Set goals in the different categories of your life including finance, relationships, health, and career. Your imagination stretches your definition of the possible.

As Oliver Wendell Holmes stated, "A man's mind stretched to a new idea can never go back to its original dimension." When I first started my career, I didn't realize that people wouldn't believe in me if I didn't believe in myself. The first sales proposal I made was for a few hundred dollars. At the time, it seemed like a large amount of money to me and I had a hard time believing they would spend it on my little ol' proposal. No surprise, they didn't. Why would they? Two decades later, my understanding of "possible" is now a hundred *million* dollars. I got to this place in my career only after learning to believe in myself and the value I was bringing with my company's resources.

Maybe I was lucky. Indeed, I feel very fortunate. However, as Roman philosopher Seneca stated, "Luck is what happens when preparation meets opportunity." And, I'll add, opportunity is there all the time!

In *Think and Grow Rich*, Napoleon Hill explains, "First comes thought; then organization of that thought into ideas and plans; then transformation of those plans into reality. The beginning, as you will observe, is in your imagination."

It all starts in your imagination.

2.6 Instructions — List Your Be, Do, & Have Goals

Take out a piece of lined paper and at the top write, "What do I want to be, do, or have over the next twenty years?" Challenge yourself to answer this question in list form and write nonstop for five minutes. Write as quickly as possible, listing one item and moving on to the next.

Below are the main categories your goals can fall under:

1) Physical
2) Mental
3) Financial
4) Career
5) Relationships
6) Experiences and Travel
7) Possessions

Next, select one major goal that would have a greater impact on your life than any other on the list. Oftentimes this may be a financial or career goal. To increase your belief, paint a clear mental picture of your desired end state. Write a paragraph about you and your life soon after having achieved this goal. The more you believe, the more likely it will become a reality.

2.7 Become a Millionaire

One of my goals was to become a millionaire. It took years of disciplined savings and forgoing immediate pleasures. Every month for over twenty years, I calculated my current assets (401(k), Roth IRA, checking and savings accounts, etc.) and liabilities (mortgage, credit card balance, student loans, etc.). By tracking these, I kept my goal in front of me to remind me to make the necessary trade-offs. The rewards were well worth it.

When I first started my professional career in 1998, my salary was $38,500. I set a goal to earn $100,000. After reaching it almost a decade later, I raised my sights and set higher goals. Despite my initial lack of belief, I set a goal that seemed outrageously unobtainable: "I will earn $300,000 in a year." This is about eight times as much as I earned when I started. I challenged myself on what it would take to accomplish this. I needed to become more valuable by adding more value to my organization and others. *If I create enough value, then the marketplace will reward me.* I studied the compensation plan of my organization and determined what it would take to achieve this goal.

Previously, my thoughts had been scattered and unfocused. Now, I was laser-focused on what I could create and do in a limited amount of time. This changed my whole perspective.

When a new opportunity was presented, I weighed its relative merits versus what I already was pursuing and determined where it would fall in terms of priority. I constantly reevaluated the top opportunities, always asking if they deserved to remain on top. I would pursue all necessary actions in order to take advantage of the top opportunity. When that was exhausted, I would move on to the second-highest-ranked opportunity. Then, onto the third and likewise down the line. By taking prioritized massive action, I ensured I was doing everything possible to achieve my major financial goal.

Once a week I would ask myself, "Which opportunity, if it were to close it, will make the biggest impact on my organization?" I calculated Weight Value as follows:

Weight Value (Impact) = Value of Closing x Probability of Closing

Weight Value: The overall factored impact for me and my organization.

Value of Closing: A project's financial merits in terms of volume and margin while also taking into account its strategic value.

Probability of Closing: The likelihood we'll reach an agreement taking into account the Timing Factor. There is no value for a project that doesn't happen.

Timing Factor: The date an agreement is expected to be reached. Often this goes with Probability of Closing. The closer we get to a closing date, the higher the Probability of Closing.

Amazingly enough, when you're laser-focused, you attract better opportunities and recognize them more efficiently. As a result, when I was introduced to an account that many others had already been introduced to and passed on, I jumped on it. This single account led me to achieving my financial goal.

What do you do when you achieve your goal? Set a new one, of course! After achieving, it's natural and normal to feel a bit down or directionless, but choose to continue to grow and stretch yourself. You're only on this earth for a limited amount of days. What will you do to leave it in a better place because you existed?

2.8 Tend Your Garden

Once, when I was gardening, I pulled weeds. Lots of weeds. I had neglected the flowerbeds for so long that the weeds had taken over. I've gone through the same routine every year. I put down mulch in the early spring hoping to prevent weeds from sprouting up. Invariably, the weeds come, and I have to pull them. The mind is in many ways like this fertile ground. My challenge has been that I keep trying unsuccessfully to keep the flower garden free of weeds without planting anything desirable. The soil is fertile, so it will be utilized by stray seeds and weeds.

Likewise, in your mind, when you choose not to plant the seeds and desires of what you *do* want, you allow a space for others to deposit seeds or weeds in your mind. The best defense is to plant that which

DAD'S LITTLE BOOK OF WISDOM

you *do* want. These desirable plants or flowers will utilize the nutrients and the sunlight and thus crowd out the weeds, preventing them from growing in the first place. Your garden will certainly still require maintenance; however, it will be easier to maintain without as many weeds. And it will yield a beautiful scene to boot!

2.9 Schedule Your Goal

> *"The moment one definitely commits oneself, then providence moves too. All sorts of things occur to help one that would never otherwise have occurred ... unforeseen incidents, meetings, and material assistance, which no man could have dreamed would have come his way."*
> — *William Hutchison Murray, Scottish mountaineer*

Once your goal is set down in writing, you need to put it on the calendar. A goal without a deadline is just a wish. Many people are afraid to set a date out of fear that they'll miss the deadline. *Overcome* this. More important than having the right deadline is generating movement and *momentum*!

Determine how much time the next activities will take. Schedule them and then resolve to do them. Do this by breaking your goals into activities and placing them in your calendar.

It helps to remember the acronym **K.I.S.S.** when scheduling your goals: **K**eep **I**t **S**imple **S**illy. Don't overcomplicate it.

One of the first steps is to simply plan and allocate your time. If you have a week, three hours, or fifteen minutes, you can determine how to best allocate that time to achieve your goal.

Break down your financial goals into monthly and annual numbers. For example, decide your annual income goal or net worth at the end of three years. Then go to work to make it a reality. By "beginning with the end in mind," you'll be more likely to reach your financial targets.

2.10 Keep Going

> *"If one advances confidently in the direction of his dreams, ... he will meet with a success unexpected in common hours."*
> — *Henry David Thoreau*

It's important to stay focused. I discovered that you can achieve almost any goal you set for yourself if you have the discipline to pay the price, to do what you need to do, and never give up.

Whatever you focus on grows. The best part is you get to choose where you focus.

I'm a big fan of Pastor Harry Emerson Fosdick's view that, "No horse gets anywhere until he is harnessed. No steam or gas ever drives anything until it is confined. No Niagara is ever turned into light and power until it is tunneled. No life ever grows great until it is focused, dedicated, disciplined."

It's one thing to know the goal and quite another to work toward it. So, keep your eye on the prize and keep working away. One way to do this is to break down goals into smaller, incremental ones. Then reward yourself for accomplishing them along the way. For example, it may be difficult for you to make a certain phone call. Declare that you will allow yourself a reward like eating a cookie, calling a friend, or reading for a few minutes following the successful dial of the phone call. It removes the focus of your mind off the fear and onto the reward.

Remind yourself of what you may receive in accomplishing your goal. This will provide you the fuel to keep it up!

It takes focus. Laser focus.

Tracking your progress helps. I have found that using a journal to write down my goals, goal plans, and progress provides the day-by-day incentive that enables them to become a reality.

While staying locked-in is beneficial, be careful of the busyness trap. When we are too busy to reflect on how we are living our lives, It's almost certain we are not busy doing the right things.

Once a year, go back and evaluate your goals and make sure they are still meaningful and accurate for you.

2.11 Overcome Your Obstacles

"You measure the size of the accomplishment by the obstacles you have to overcome to reach your goals."
— *Booker T. Washington*

When you're committed to a goal or outcome, providence will make a way. It's amazing how creative you can be once you put your mind to it.

Can you recall a time when you had a nervous, apprehensive sensation in your stomach while attempting something new? This may actually be signaling you're on the right track. John Maxwell advises, "Reaching new goals and moving to a higher level of performance always requires change, and change feels awkward. But take comfort in the knowledge that if a change doesn't feel uncomfortable, it's probably not a real change."

What can get in the way of you achieving your dream? Lukewarm motivation. If you don't have a strong enough *why,* you'll be tempted to stop or give up. But when the *why* becomes big enough, the *how* becomes easy.

Failure will never overtake you if your desire to succeed is strong enough. Why? Because you'll keep trying. In the movie *Rocky Balboa*, Rocky tells his son, "But it ain't about how hard you hit, it's about how hard you can *get* hit and keep moving forward."

I'll share another example of an elite athlete overcoming great odds — this time an Olympian.

In February 2018, snowboarder Shaun White stood atop the half-pipe at the PyeongChang Winter Olympics awaiting the signal that would start his third and final run. Four years of training and effort would come down to this one last final performance.

After all the other competitors completed their runs, White felt confident he would finish with no less than a silver medal. But he hadn't tirelessly trained and overcome obstacles to come in second. He trailed 19-year-old rising star Ayumu Hirano and needed a virtually flawless performance to win gold.

He delivered.

With stunning back-to-back 1440s, he finished with a final run of 97.75 to earn his third gold medal.

What can we take away from Shaun White's gold-medal performance to use in our own lives?

Here are three takeaways:

1) Start with dreams. Turn them into goals. Fuel them with desire.
White won his first snowboarding gold medal at age 19 and his second at age 23. He was at the top of his profession. When he finished fourth at age 27 at the 2014 Olympics, many thought he'd be on the way to retirement. White thought otherwise, and would prove it four years later. Bud Keene, who coached White to Olympic gold medals in 2006 and 2010, said, "He's taken it three levels from where he started."

2) Keep pushing.
I believe it must be daunting to train for four years knowing that a single performance will define your efforts. How do Olympians do it? Many ultra-successful athletes and professionals credit their wins to establishing helpful daily habits. For White, this rigorous pursuit of his best meant waking up each day at 6 a.m., spending two hours in the gym, five hours training, two hours meeting with his coaches, and two hours watching practice footage before collapsing into bed at midnight and then starting his routine all over again.

3) Persevere through obstacles.
In October 2017, three months before the 2018 Olympics, White was snowboarding in New Zealand on a training run. He took off early on a double cork 1440 and came down too hard, slapping the edge of the

half-pipe at an awkward angle. Then it got worse.

After the initial impact, his board dug in and whipped him forward, face-first, into the icy surface. Blood ran across the snow. A helicopter was summoned. White was rushed to a hospital. It took sixty-two stitches to close a jagged gash across his forehead and mend the tip of his tongue. That was four months before the Olympics. He didn't quit. He overcame both his fourth-place finish and a gruesome injury to win the 2018 gold medal.

Next time you're ready to give up on your goal, remember Shaun White to help you push yourself to new heights.

2.12 Instructions — Use Affirmations

Affirmations are one of the techniques I use to achieve my goals. Follow these three steps to make best use of affirmations:

1. Write out a statement of your desire.

Read it aloud *at least* two times a day: once in the morning when you wake up and once at night before you go to bed. Look yourself in the mirror and don't worry about what your spouse or others may think.

2. Record yourself making this statement.

Use your phone to record yourself making the statement.

3. Listen to the recording as you drive.

The more you recite it and hear it, the deeper you push it into your subconscious. Recall the analogy of your mind as a garden; by listening to what you desire to become, you'll fill your garden with seeds of the person you will become.

I originally dismissed this approach when I first heard about it in *Think and Grow Rich*. For years I didn't follow it. This changed when I had a sales coach to keep me accountable, and it helped me find success. Then I applied this formula to achieve an annual income goal that was multiple times what I had earned prior. It helped to condition my mind to recognize opportunities that I then acted upon. I strongly urge you to try it.

2.13 Get to the Finish Line — Part II

When I decided to go for my own version of the gold and qualify for the Boston Marathon by running the Philadelphia Marathon, I was juiced and excited! For context, in 2008 there were 45 million runners in the U.S. and less than 1 percent of them had run a marathon.

I thought I had done everything right: I knew exactly what I wanted. I had a plan that had been shaped by mentors; I had put in over six months of consistently running thirty to forty miles a week; and I honestly believed I could do it. So, when race day came, I carefully followed my plan. When I got to mile 13, I was on pace and felt great! I just knew I was going to do it. However, by mile 20, I no longer felt so confident and I was losing steam. The best way I can describe myself during the last six miles is like a car running out of gas. I knew what I needed to do but couldn't get my body to respond. I finished the race in 3 hours and 13 minutes, missing the qualification time by only three minutes!

I realized in the aftermath that sometimes you learn more from defeat than you do from success. I quickly went over what went wrong, and with the help of my fellow runners I identified three things I could change to improve my time. First, I needed to take in nutrition during the race in the form of gel packs. Second, I'd enhance my endurance by increasing from forty to over fifty miles a week. Finally, I'd enlist a pace group to prevent me from going out too fast. At the time, my wife had encouraging words for me: "Mark, you're never going to be in this good of shape again. This is your opportunity. If you want to do this, then do it now." That evening we found another marathon about eight weeks away where I could try to qualify again. I ran the Houston Marathon in 3 hours and 7 minutes, this time qualifying by three minutes!

★ ★ ★

Once you clarify your goals, you can finally take action on the smaller achievements needed to get there. There will be obstacles and it will likely be harder than you imagined, but remind yourself that your goals are your truest desires, and that you can achieve them.

Adopting the right mindset is often harder than any physical task you will be asked to perform. I'll show you how to adopt a winning attitude in the next chapter.

Take Action

☐ Use the SMART system to create your goal.

☐ Don't tell everyone. Instead adopt the motto, "Don't tell the world. Show it."

☐ Set goals for different parts of your life. What do you want to be, do, and have?

☐ Schedule your goals and revisit them often.

☐ Begin daily affirmations.

☐ Don't be afraid to stand out.

Read These Books:

☐ *The ONE Thing* by Gary W. Keller and Jay Papasan

☐ *Goals!* by Brian Tracy

☐ *See You at the Top* by Zig Ziglar

3

ADJUST YOUR ATTITUDE

"It is your attitude, more than your aptitude, that will determine your altitude."

Zig Ziglar

Adjusting your attitude to enjoy the hard work is an integral part of achieving any goal. So, today, choose to be an optimist. Optimism is more associated with success and happiness than any other quality. This is because without a positive belief that a situation may work out, you may give up before you even begin. Because so many people are pessimistic, it makes it easier for the optimists to succeed with continual and persistent action. Be one of them.

St. Ignatius is an excellent example of this. He advised, "Always work as though everything depended on you. Yet always pray knowing that everything depends on God."

When I was a regional sales and marketing director, my company had an internal competition to see which of our roughly fifty areas would be able to deliver the best results. The highest scoring area fell under my territory. When I asked my area sales manager what they were doing to achieve the top results, he replied, "Mark, we will not be denied. We have an attitude that everyone who calls in is looking for the right fit, and we'll provide it! We have armed our team with several options. If the initial ones are not palatable to the customer, we have other options. Our team members believe in themselves and the product, and it has led to these stellar results."

Optimism promotes an attitude of continual improvement. To make a better future, you will naturally focus on improving. What you were not able to perform yesterday, perhaps you will be capable of today or tomorrow.

This chapter will help you develop a very powerful attitude. It's one I have tried to adopt for the better part of the past eight years. I only wish

I had understood and applied what I'm sharing with you here earlier in my career.

3.1 Welcome Hard Work

Hard work is one of the secrets to success. Don't be someone who tries to find a way to reach success without paying your dues. You can try, but you should know it just doesn't happen that way. In fact, it's the opposite. Those who are trying to shirk work will find themselves saddled with working longer later in their life and having more of a difficult time than those who are willing to embrace hard work. How can this be so? Let me illustrate.

A hired worker was bragging to a colleague, "I get in a bit late, take a long lunch, and am able to sneak out a bit early. Near as I can tell, I'm working half a day and getting paid for the full day. I got it made!"

Little did the hired hand know that because of his slacking, his employer was just keeping him on until he could hire a new, harder-working person before letting him go. This soon-to-be-fired individual will then find it a bit harder to gain new employment, as prospective employers will wonder why he was let go so quickly. Some serious belt tightening may be in his future until he can obtain another job. Will he learn his lesson? Unfortunately, the odds are not in his favor. More likely than not, he will blame his "bad luck" on external factors rather than taking full accountability. By choosing to do less work, he has brought upon himself a harder life.

By contrast, a cheerful worker who welcomes doing the hard work with a pleasant attitude will likely find themselves employed and in high demand. They'll also reduce their likelihood of being laid off if their company falls on hard times.

Bill Gates's dad was wealthy, so he was sent to a private school for wealthy kids. In 1968, the school's Moms Club bought computer terminal time for the students. This resulted in Gates programming well before many colleges *even had* computers. A mother of a student at his high school engaged the computer club for a new payroll company, and Gates was hired. The result was free programming time for Gates. In 1971, Gates and a friend did 1,575 hours over seven months. This is equivalent to eight hours a day, 7 days a week for 7 months! By his sophomore year at Harvard, he had well over ten years of experience programming. His hard work put him well ahead of others in this new industry.

3.2 Exercise Self-Discipline

> *"The ability to discipline yourself to delay gratification in the short term, in order to enjoy greater rewards in the long term, is the indispensable prerequisite for success."*
> — *Brian Tracy*

Motivational speaker Brian Tracy shared a story of how early in his career he was at a conference and sat down for lunch with an older gentleman and his assistant. It turns out the man was an author who had written four books each containing over 250 success principles. Tracy asked him, "Out of all the 1,000 success principles that you have learned, what is the most important?" With a twinkle in his eye, recognizing he had heard that question many times, he responded, "Out of all the success principles I've studied, the most important is self-discipline. Self-discipline is the ability to do *what* you need to do, *when* you need to do it, whether you *feel like it or not*. With self-discipline, all the other principles will work. Without self-discipline, none of them will work."

In order to accomplish anything worthwhile, you must have the self-discipline to do what you should do, regardless of whether you feel like it or not. Let me say that again: *in order to accomplish anything worthwhile, you must have the self-discipline to do what you should do, regardless of whether you feel like it or not.*

Discipline is the bridge between goals and accomplishments. Discipline is doing what you *don't* want to do, so you can later do what you *do* want to do.

How do you practice discipline? Remember what you want every morning. Keep that vision of why you're working hard in your mind's eye. Fan the flames of your desire. If your *why* is big enough, you can muster the discipline to take the necessary action.

3.3 Do or Do Not

When asked about his genius, and how he could file more patents than any other person alive, Thomas Edison replied, "None of my inventions came by accident. I see a worthwhile need to be met and I make trial after trial until it comes. What it boils down to is 1 percent inspiration and 99 percent perspiration." Many people have ideas for products, but 99 out of 100 will not take action. It's the action and ability to keep taking action that separates Edison from those "would-be-inventors."

In *The Empire Strikes Back*, as Luke Skywalker struggles to use the force to lift his X-Wing out of the bog, he complains to Yoda that he is trying, but it's just too big and too hard. Yoda replies, "Do. Or do not. There is no try."

Next time you face a difficult task and are tempted to claim you'll "try," picture Yoda's 900-year-old wrinkled face instructing you. You may choose to rephrase your statements of doubt to be one of confidence. From "I will *try* to write a book" to "I *will* write a page a day until I have written one hundred pages." You can choose your actions, and you can choose to continue taking action until you achieve the outcome you desire. The choice is yours.

Recently, I was invited to throw axes with a friend. I was pretty good at it, and did quite well. Until I didn't. I went absolutely stone-cold near the end. I resolved that we weren't leaving until I ended on a bull's-eye. Every time I threw it, not only could I not hit the bull's-eye, I couldn't even get it to stick on the board. This got into my head. The more I "tried," the more difficult it became. I was thinking about lowering my standards to just getting an ax to stick on the board again, but then I relaxed and reminded myself I could do it. I had already done it several times before, I just needed to experiment to get out of my funk. Sure enough, on one of my next throws, I threw a perfect bull's-eye! I took a picture and we left.

What I needed was resolve. As Dr. Wayne Dyer said "There is no scarcity of opportunity to make a living at what you love to do; there is only scarcity of resolve to make it happen." Choose with care, and then resolve not to *try*, but to *do*.

3.4 Work to the Best of Your Ability

Early in my career, I used to shun work, and my demeanor would sour when faced with a large amount of effort without a guaranteed reward. I didn't want to "waste my time" on clients who weren't going to buy. I wanted to do the minimum amount of work and reap the maximum rewards. "Do less and earn more" may be a great sound bite for someone selling a get-rich-quick scheme, but I found it to be an unrewarding philosophy. I started to realize that whether I worked hard or not hard at all, a year later I would simply be a year older. Time didn't care. However, my experience and value came from work compounded over time.

When my attitude about hard work changed, I found I could actually enjoy a certain portion of my tasks. With every client I encountered, I gained experience and was able to continue tailoring and refining my offerings so that they could suit the next client. Correspondingly, my productivity skyrocketed. The more I worked, within reason, the happier I felt, and the more rewards I received. Actively choosing to go into the task even made them easier to do.

This is consistent with what philosopher Thomas Carlyle discovered, "The most unhappy of all men is the man that cannot tell what he is going to do, that has got no work cut out for him in the world. ... For work is the grand cure of all the maladies and miseries that ever beset mankind — honest work which you intend getting done."

There is a minimum contribution that's expected. It's the amount of effort and value you put in *above* this level that will set you apart from the rest. Doing the minimum amount may seem like the easy path, but it's not. Doing the minimum amount leads to being seen as a commodity and no more valuable than all the rest. As Henry David Thoreau wrote, "Drive a nail home and clinch it so faithfully that you can wake up in the night and think of your work with satisfaction."

3.5 Maintain Integrity and Build Trust

Warren Buffett didn't become the richest man in the world by just buying *some* stock; he would buy *entire companies*. When asked what he looked for in the people and companies he invested in, he responded, "In looking for people to hire, look for three qualities: integrity, intelligence, and energy. But if they don't have the first, the other two will kill you."

Integrity is part of what it takes to be trustworthy.

In the Bible, Jesus shared the relationship between work and trust, stating, "Well done, good and faithful servant. You have done well in small matters. I will entrust you with larger ones." He also said, "The person who is trustworthy in very small matters is also trustworthy in great ones; and the person who is dishonest in very small matters is also dishonest in great ones."

This is how life works. If you handle your responsibilities well and demonstrate a willingness to take on more, you will be handed more responsibility. But those who cheat when people aren't looking will continue to be dishonest in greater matters.

At one point in my sales career, I was told over and over about the importance of developing relationships with customers, yet I struggled to do so. It felt manipulative to me. Was I going to buddy up to someone so they would feel obligated to buy from me? I rejected this tactic.

Then I read Stephen M.R. Covey's *The Speed of Trust.* In it, he discusses how relationships are built by being liked and trusted. He further explains that "Trust is a function of two things: character and competence. Character includes your integrity, your motive, your intent with people. Competence includes your capabilities, your skills, your results, your track record."

Once I understood that in every interaction I was either building or destroying trust, I changed my mindset and behavior and never looked back. My sales, career, income, and life enjoyment all took a sharp turn for the better. Does your career rely on building relationships with others? If so, I strongly urge you to pick up a copy of Covey's book.

3.6 GOYA!

How do you get yourself to take action when you don't feel like it? One method I frequently employ is saying a mantra out loud to kick-start me into the right frame of mind and then to act. One of my favorite mantras is based on Newton's Laws of Motion: "A body in motion tends to stay in motion. A body at rest tends to stay at rest." Or as I like to say, "GOYA!" GOYA stands for "Get Off Your Ass!"

To spur action, I also think of Wayne Gretzky's famous line: "You miss 100 percent of the shots you don't take." When you have an opportunity, take the shot! Don't worry about the magnitude of an undertaking. Just take action.

Don't worry about failing or not being good enough. Anything worth doing is worth doing poorly until you develop your skill enough to perform with excellence.

3.7 Subordinate Your Dislike for Your Purpose

Next time you're tempted to say, "Yes, *but I don't want to* _____!" catch yourself and remember these words by Albert E.N. Gray: "The successful person has the habit of doing the things failures don't like to do. They don't like doing them either, but their disliking is subordinated to the strength of their purpose."

Keep your mind magnetized on where you're going. This will allow you to overlook the many trivial things that would otherwise trip you up. Remain focused squarely on achieving what you want to accomplish.

Some of your goals may remain elusive. That's why maintaining a healthy attitude while consistently taking action is so important. John F. Kennedy boldly stated, "There are risks and costs to a program of action. But they are far less than the long-range risks and costs of comfortable inaction." I've adopted the mental attitude that failure is not about an individual sales opportunity, but about not being able to reach my goals at all. Compete against the clock, because the time will pass regardless of what you choose to do. A year from now, it will be a year from now. What will you do to give yourself the greatest chance of succeeding?

It's not how you feel that determines how you act. It's how you act that determines how you feel. The wonderful thing is that you can control the actions you take! Success is connected with action. Successful men and women keep moving. They make mistakes, but they don't quit. With enough enthusiasm and energy, you can persevere to complete any worthy undertaking.

3.8 Persist

> *"Nothing in the world can take the place of persistence.*
> *Talent will not ... Genius will not ... Education will not ...*
> *Persistence and determination alone are omnipotent."*
> — *President Calvin Coolidge*

Whatever your goal is, persistence is vital to seeing your desires through. Below are five areas where a persistent attitude will pay off:

1. Persist for the long term
2. Persist to the finish
3. Persist to overcome failure
4. Persist with a strong mental focus
5. Persist to boost your luck

Let's dig into each of these. I'll use a real example to illustrate.

1. Persist for the Long Term

As I write this, I just came back from a run. I used to run a lot more, but since I'm out of practice and this was twice as long as any run I have done over the past year, it was really hard. But I've run marathons eight times the length of what I just ran. While physically I'm out of practice, mentally I recall what it was like and what I need to do to get back in shape. Everything is hard before it becomes easy. I know that these distances will soon be easy to run.

Steel magnate Andrew Carnegie believed that "anything in life worth having is worth working for." True to form, virtually every success story involves someone or some group working harder than the others. Success comes down to persistence.

In his book *Outliers*, Malcolm Gladwell posited the "10,000-Hour Rule." The rule simply states that it takes 10,000 hours of practice and application to achieve mastery of a craft or skill. While other musical groups were performing an hour or two a week, in the early years the Beatles played continuously for eight or more hours a day, day after day, racking up playing experience. During their off time, they created more songs. They poured in hours early and it made their career skyrocket later.

Remember how young Bill Gates was provided an early opportunity to work on computers when it was very expensive to do so. He had 10,000 hours of computer programming time before he dropped out of college to form Microsoft.

Do you desire to entertain millions with a comedy routine, write a book that reaches the hearts of its readers, or design a beautiful house? Each of these are examples of aspirations that require you to achieve some level of mastery of your field.

If you dedicate four hours a day toward a vital skill for five days a week, that's twenty hours a week. If you maintain that for fifty weeks a year, you will reach 10,000 hours in ten years. This is why mastery doesn't happen overnight but after a sustained effort.

Writer William Feather observed, "Success seems to be largely a matter of hanging on after others have let go." The richest man of his day, John D. Rockefeller, agreed with him: "I do not think there is any other quality so essential to success of any kind as the quality of perseverance. It overcomes almost everything, even nature."

I once pulled an all-nighter to submit a proposal for my start-up company when I believed it had the opportunity to be the break we needed to win a marquee project. This followed weeks of intense work and phone calls by me and our team.

I knew that unless we had sales results soon, the parent company would need to let people go or just shut us down. I was grateful that one of my colleagues was with me until 10:00 p.m. before heading for home, but I knew there was a lot more work to go if we were going to even have a chance. That was one of the longest nights of my life.

What is it that you want? Have you set your goal and sights? Making it a reality will depend on your work ethic and ability to stay on task.

2. Persist to the Finish

You never fail until you stop trying. The person who says, "I will do this *until* ..." finds a way. As Abraham Lincoln stated, "Always bear in mind that your resolution to succeed is more important than any other thing."

At my start-up company, the night that I pulled the all-nighter solidified my resolve for the success of our business unit. It also demonstrated my dedication to the rest of our team in a way that no words ever could.

I *needed* to finish before I would end the night. I methodically created content and edited it to address all of the client's requested categories. When my boss came in the next day, he innocently asked, "Oh Mark, what time did you guys end last night?" I looked up from my computer at him with my bleary eyes and just shook my head. His eyes widened with the realization I had never left. I looked down and returned to typing.

As others came into the office that day, my boss had them ask me what I needed to finish. The entire team helped with the printing and assembling of ten required binders. A colleague volunteered to drive the three hours to submit it, which would have it arriving with less than an hour to spare. When he hopped in his car, I went home and crashed on my bed. While we didn't end up winning the job, in a sense it didn't matter: success is in the trying. Best of all, following this event, I felt the rest of the people around me choosing to step up their own personal commitment levels so we could all succeed.

Leaving projects unresolved will drain your confidence and motivation. William James observed, "Nothing is so fatiguing as the eternal hanging on of an uncompleted task." Resolve to complete what you start and don't take on more than you can complete. From time to time, you may find yourself overwhelmed. Make a decision to either complete the tasks or shed some obligations. Either way, you'll feel peace of mind in the persistence.

Theodore Roosevelt proclaimed the following:

> "It is not the critic who counts; not the man who points out how the strong man stumbles, or where the doer of deeds could have done them better. The credit belongs to the man who is actually in the arena, whose face is marred by dust and sweat and blood; who strives valiantly; who errs, who comes up short again and again ... ; who knows great enthusiasms, the great devotions; who spends himself in a worthy cause; who at the best knows in the end the triumph of high achievement, and who at the worst, if he fails, at least fails while daring greatly, so that his place shall never be with those cold and timid souls who neither know victory nor defeat."

Be willing to enter the arena!

3. Persist to Overcome Failure

Winners are just losers who got up and gave it one more try. It hurts to fail, but it hurts more to have never tried to succeed.

On July 6, 1928, Otto Rohwedder rolled out an invention that would slice bread. Did the people of his day recognize him as a genius and beat a path to his door to buy his invention? Hardly. Could they predict that a century later people would often refer to great inventions as the "greatest thing since sliced bread"? No, because it was a total failure.

It wasn't until the machine was later effectively marketed that people accepted sliced bread. Those who try something and fail are infinitely better than those who try nothing and succeed. They have successfully gained experience. Failed attempts are the real keys to learning.

You need not fear making mistakes. Despite failing to achieve the outcome you desire, persisting can help you overcome your obstacles. A person who has never made a mistake has never tried anything new and probably never achieved their goals. *Pay as little attention as possible to those who would discourage you.* Rather, focus your whole self and energy into making your endeavor a reality. A ship may encounter rocky waves on its voyage to reach the harbor on the other side, but no matter how many waves of opposition it may encounter, it will not turn back.

Once, a reporter asked Thomas Edison, "Have you really failed 10,000 times to make the incandescent electric light bulb?" Edison responded, "No, young man, I have not failed. I have successfully found 10,000 ways not to make the light bulb." His attitude made all the difference.

One summer in my teenage years, a friend of mine invited me and a number of friends out to his lake house. We went out on the family's speedboat to learn how to ski. My first time in the water, my friend's dad called out from the boat, "Sit back and let the rope do the work. Don't lean forward." Unfortunately, I was too hardheaded. I kept feeling the urge to pull myself up. Time after time I was rewarded with falling face first into the water. After several unsuccessful attempts, I was called back into the boat to allow another person to try. She got up on her third attempt. I got back in the water and tried again. Again and again I failed. I resolved I would not leave the lake until I successfully was able to water-ski. Finally, I got up and onto my skis — it only took twenty-six times!

4. Persist with a Strong Mental Focus

My wife, son, and I all enjoyed seeing the Broadway production of *Hamilton* when it came to Philadelphia. It's an incredible story about the life of Alexander Hamilton, who created the United States treasury and was George Washington's right-hand man, acclaimed for his intellectual feats. He provided insight into his celebrated brilliance: "Men give me some credit for genius. All the genius I have lies just in this: when I have a subject in hand, I study it profoundly. Day and night, it is before me. ... My mind becomes pervaded with it." Do you wish to be considered a genius? You now know the formula. Dig into your problems and stay with them longer.

Much of success is a mental game. It's a fascinating truth: if you refuse to accept anything but the best, you very often get it. You attract into your life what you think about. Former Treasury Secretary George Shultz recognized this fact: "The minute you start talking about what you're going to do if you lose, you have lost."

Adopt an attitude of gratitude for the ability to perform your work, do it to the best of your ability, and be prepared mentally to put in the necessary effort. Noted playwright George Bernard Shaw provided a solid road map that I have sought to emulate. He recalled, "When I was young, I observed that nine of ten things I did were failures, so I did ten times the work."

This was my plan. I resolved to see ten, fifty, or one hundred customers until we won one.

With the team committed we also brought in top engineering talent — someone with experience and expertise that was sorely needed. I learned a ton from him. I also learned from writing that failed proposal and the many others that followed. Each time I didn't feel lost sales were failures because I was learning and the team was refining our message. I knew we'd succeed if we just had enough time.

5. Persist to Boost Your Luck

Successful people are very lucky, just ask any failure! The truth is, there is no secret to success. It takes hard work, commitment, plus a little bit of luck. But those who give 100 percent every day tend to have more *luck* than others. *The harder you work, the luckier you'll become.* The more you work, the more you put yourself out there, and the more opportunities you'll get for luck to shine on you.

Finally, when another potential opportunity came in that could have been assigned to someone else, my boss chose for it to go to me. I like to think that was because I earned his confidence and that I represented the best chance for our team's success.

Luck is when opportunity meets preparedness, and opportunity is there all the time.

3.9 Face Your Fears

We all face fear in one form or another. Does asking your employer for the day off to take care of your family's needs scare you? Do butterflies fill your stomach prior to sending a difficult email or text message? Do you feel trepidation before you have to place an unpleasant call? These are all common examples of fear taking over.

If you're worried that your deepest fears will come true, odds are they won't. In a 2019 Penn State study, researchers Lucas LaFreniere and Michelle Newman had twenty-nine anxious people write down their worries over a ten-day period, review them every night, and note the severity of their worries.

Twenty days later, they were asked how many of them had come true. Significantly, 91.4 percent of the worry predictions did not come true. Keep this in mind next time you begin to worry. Less than one out of every ten fears you have may come true.

To help you remember, use this acronym for **FEAR:**

F – False
E – Evidence
A – Appearing
R – Real

When you have an unpleasant task to do, the best approach is simply to resolve to do it first! Use the motto, "Feared things first!" Then begin right where you are to do some small portion of it. Begin writing the email. Pick up the phone and begin dialing. Just begin! After you're done, regardless of the outcome, you'll feel proud of yourself for taking action. You'll oftentimes find that it wasn't nearly as bad as you may have originally thought.

Want more evidence? Conduct your own experiment using a Decision Tracker that I'll discuss in Chapter 7.

This wisdom has been shared in many forms over the years. Ralph Waldo Emerson advised, "Don't be too timid and squeamish about your actions. All life is an experiment. The more experiments you make, the better" and "Do the thing you fear and the death of fear is certain."

Is **FEAR** still preventing you from taking action? Imagine you've just been selected to be on a TV show that would be the thrill of a lifetime but would force you out of your comfort zone. Would you go?

The Amazing Race is a popular TV show that my wife and I enjoyed watching. Contestants had to race to some remote corner of the world, find the designated station, perform the challenge, earn a clue, and then begin the process all over again. Those who did it had to throw their whole hearts in to succeed. This was so entertaining to watch because it's contrary to how most of us live our daily lives. Phil Keoghan, the host of *The Amazing Race*, noted, "As a society, we've stopped taking risk in our lives. We've started living in fear. We're so busy obsessing over our restrictions that we've become scared to fully live."

Are you afraid to make mistakes? Perhaps that's because of school conditioning that raised you to try to be perfect. In school there were "right" answers. If you were good at memorizing or performing the math function, you could earn good grades. The real world is much more complex. Interacting with people is not an exact science. Instead, it's a more prudent course of action to attempt, fail, learn, and then make another attempt. As psychologist Henry C. Link observed, "While one person hesitates because he feels inferior, the other is busy making mistakes and becoming superior."

What was the attitude and mindset of one of the greatest basketball players ever to play? Michael Jordan, winner of six NBA finals, said:

DAD'S LITTLE BOOK OF WISDOM

"There was never any fear for me, no fear of failure. If I missed a shot, so what? I can rationalize the fact that there are only two outcomes: You either make it, or you miss it. I could think that way because I had earned the opportunity to take that shot. I had put in all the work, not only in that particular game, but in practice every day. If I missed, then it wasn't meant to be. You are the sum total of all the work you have put in, nothing more and nothing less. If you are confident you have done everything possible to prepare yourself, then there is nothing to fear. It just wasn't meant to be."

That's so powerful I'm going to repeat it! *If you are confident you have done everything possible to prepare yourself, then there is nothing to fear. It just wasn't meant to be.*

We think we will die of embarrassment if we are rejected. We sometimes don't even get up to bat because we don't want to strike out. The way I understand it, success and failure, as commonly spoken of, are really impostors. It's the experience of moving toward the goal that's true success. Moving equals success. *Not* moving equals failure.

Here is a fun little poem that serves as a reminder of the danger of adopting a limiting mindset:

Beware of those who stand aloof
And greet each venture with reproof;
The world would stop if things were run
By men who say, "It can't be done."

Finally, what you think of yourself is much more important than what others think of you. Guard your opinion of yourself very carefully.

3.10 Find Your Right Fit
One of the discoveries I found most helpful in my life was that I didn't need to measure myself against someone else's definition of success.

However, by reading this, I hope to spare you from the years it took for me to learn this.

After graduating from college and accepting my first job, I was eager to succeed. I wished to emulate the person I believed I should be like. Unfortunately, this meant leaving my personality at home and adopting what I thought was a professional approach. True, I was professional, but I also became much more like a robot without truly connecting with people. I didn't enjoy it, and ultimately the marketplace didn't connect with me either.

Later, a mentor showed me that business and sales success didn't require me to leave my individuality at home. I found that others warmed up to me, I enjoyed my work much more, and lo and behold, the business success came flowing in!

You have talents and abilities that are unique and different from those around you. Learn from those who have gone before you, but don't mistakenly believe that you have to be exactly like them. If you're more of an introvert, accept this about yourself, and realize that many of the world's successful leaders are wired this way, including Abraham Lincoln, Dwight D. Eisenhower, Bill Gates, Mark Zuckerberg, and Steven Spielberg. If Apple co-founder Steve Jobs had not partnered with his introverted co-founder Steve Wozniak the world might have never heard of Steve Jobs, the Apple computer, or the iPhone. Learn about yourself. Learn what you do phenomenally well. Once you do, you may choose to set a different course for how to achieve the results you desire compared to your boisterous friend.

Early in my career, I was in a technical sales position. Meeting with facility directors to discuss their building automation system or rooftop units never truly excited me. I had to force myself to do the work. I felt like a square peg trying to fit into a round hole. As a result, I was almost fired *three times.* Why? Because I wasn't producing the results the company wanted. I was the wrong fit. I didn't realize my skills of detail orientation were thorough and methodical. It was overkill for smaller transactional sales. Later, I returned to the same company in a different position. This time, I rocketed to the top in less than eighteen months. This position was a better fit for my skills, interests, and personality.

When I was younger, I thought everyone saw the world the same way I saw it. I didn't fully appreciate my unique strengths and how to best use my talents.

What is your best fit? Are you enjoying your chosen profession? If so, great! If not, perhaps you just haven't yet found the right fit for you. I urge you to learn about your own combination of strengths and talents. Then put yourself in a position that requires them.[1]

Henry Ford stated, "The whole secret of a successful life is to find out what it is one's destiny to do, and then do it."

Similarly, a quote often attributed to Einstein reads: "Everybody is a genius. But if you judge a fish by its ability to climb a tree, it will live its whole life believing that it is stupid." Life is too short to sell yourself short. If you aren't feeling good about your contributions, examine your talents, skills, and interests. Is there a profession where you'll be able to more fully utilize these?

Of course, just having the talent is not the whole picture — far from it! You still have much work to do. A genius is a talented person who does their homework. If you're engaged in a course of action you enjoy, it's much easier to put in the time and effort. The effort performed in a cheerful and pleasant attitude will yield desirable outcomes. This is what I refer to as the Upward Spiral. Success creates success!

3.11 Get Better

Most people have the wrong attitude about work. They see work as an unpleasant task to be avoided at all costs. People trudge through life putting in minimal efforts to collect a minimal paycheck and complaining that it isn't enough. This is the wrong attitude to adopt!

The most important question to ask on the job is *not*, "What

1 Go to www.Dadslittlebookofwisdom.com
  to access a link to conduct your own assessment.

am I getting?" The most important question to ask is, "What am I becoming?" Be less concerned about what you are earning and instead be focused on what skills and capabilities you are developing. These will be *far* more valuable to you in the long run.

Jim Rohn said it well:

> "Learn to work harder on yourself than you do on your job. If you work hard on your job, you can make a living. If you work hard on yourself, you can make a fortune. If you go to work on your goals, your goals will go to work on you. If you go to work on your plan, your plan will go to work on you. Whatever good things we build end up building us. Don't wish it were easier; wish you were better. Don't wish for less problems; wish for more skills. Don't wish for less challenges; wish for more wisdom."

We often change ourselves for one of two reasons: inspiration or desperation. Do you wait until you are faced with dire circumstances? Or do you decide to make a change and go after what is possible for you?

Staying the same is impossible. The world keeps spinning and if you're standing still, you're falling behind. As basketball coach Pat Riley said, "If you are not getting better, you are getting worse."

People create their own success by learning what they need to learn and then practicing it until they become proficient. This is the attitude I adopted when I set out to learn both public speaking and writing.

My friend Cole is a respected salesman and someone I admire deeply. One day I asked him, "Cole, how have you been able to go from being a service technician to becoming one of the best salespeople in your area?" He responded, "Well, I learned that I needed to overcome my fear of speaking with big people. You know, those CEOs or VPs who carry big titles and can make the decisions for large projects that we want to sell. I was afraid to speak with them. So, I joined Toastmasters, where they had me get up in front of the group and practice speaking. Through practice, practice, practice, I got more and more comfortable speaking in front of a group of people. What I learned was that when I lost my fear of speaking in front of a group of people, I lost my fear of speaking in front of a "big" person, no matter how important their title may be."

Cole's example inspired me to join Toastmasters. It was one of the best investments of time I ever made. Does your career require you to speak in front of groups, lead meetings, or influence people? If so, I recommend joining a local Toastmasters club.[2]

When I first began writing, I was afraid to put my opinions and ideas out publicly, where they might be criticized. I told myself that I wanted to maintain a level of professionalism. Really, I was just afraid. I set a goal to write and post ten LinkedIn posts over the course of a year. This goal forced me out of my comfort zone. Today the uncomfortable feelings still exist, but through repetition, repetition, repetition, I keep taking action and find it easier each time.

As a lover of reading, one of the traps I find myself falling into at times is reading without taking action. To avoid this trap, after you read something and find yourself thinking, "That's a good idea," I recommend two steps:

1) Find a way to put it into practice immediately!
2) Teach someone else what you learned. Not only will this help cement it into your memory, it will also help the person you just shared it with.

One of the greatest satisfactions you can ever have comes from the knowledge that you can do one thing superlatively well. Learning is defined as a change in behavior. You haven't learned a thing until you take action and use it. That which we persist in doing becomes easier. The nature of the task may not have changed, but our ability has increased.

2 Go to www.Dadslittlebookofwisdom.com
   to access a link to find local Toastmasters clubs near you.

Actions that can be completed in fifteen to sixty minutes are much easier to tackle. Strung together, a series of actions requiring only an hour at a time can lead to some pretty incredible results.

3.12 Adopt Successful Habits

Why should you worry about adopting good habits? This little poem from Stephen Covey's *The 7 Habits of Highly Effective People* serves as a reminder of how your thoughts can impact your life.

> *Sow a thought, reap an action;*
> *Sow an action, reap a habit;*
> *Sow a habit, reap a character;*
> *Sow a character, reap a destiny.*

As Aristotle said, "We are what we repeatedly do." What are you doing? What are your actions and habits?

Success is nothing more than a few simple disciplines practiced every day. Motivation is what gets you started, but habits are what enable your goals to become a reality.

When we're first starting out, it's easy to be derailed. A new idea or venture is like the start of a fire. At first it may be nothing more than a single flame on a matchstick; it can be snuffed out with a single breath. After nurturing and coaxing with small twigs and then larger sticks and eventually logs, the roaring blaze could burn down a forest if unchecked. Likewise, an idea needs to be nurtured by those with *faith* and *belief*. Guard your ideas carefully. An idea may be killed in infancy by a well-meaning but skeptical person with a negative comment. An idea that grows and grows can take on a life of its own.

A habit is similar. The beginning of a habit is like an invisible thread, but every time we repeat the act, we strengthen the strand and add to it another filament, until it becomes a great cable and binds, irrevocably, thoughts and actions. A routine brings excellence within the grasp of mediocrity.

J. Paul Getty, one of the wealthiest men of his era, explained that "the individual who wants to reach the top in business must appreciate the might of the force of habit — and must understand that practices are what create habits. He must be quick to break those habits that can break him — and hasten to adopt those practices that will become the habits that help him achieve the success he desires."

3.13 Seek Mentors

I've been blessed to have a few mentors who have profoundly impacted my life. I've found mentors in bosses, colleagues, friends, and even clients. These are relationships with someone more knowledgeable and experienced than you in a certain category of life. You don't need to ask them to be your mentor. Actions will speak louder than words. Simply ask someone you respect for advice on how to handle a situation. If it sounds good, act upon it. Then go back to them and tell them, "I did what you said and this is what happened." Invest in regular time with them. Share your struggles and successes. When they care about you personally, they'll put in more time to help you. Don't let it all be one-sided. Find a way to give back to them in a meaningful way. This can be treating them to breakfast or lunch, introducing them to a potential business opportunity, or sharing an article they may enjoy.

"What do you look for when hiring people?" I asked this question of my former boss and mentor, Gerry, after being promoted into the role of regional sales and marketing director. I needed to immediately hire three new area sales managers. Gerry replied, "I look for skill and will. The 'skills' you can tell from reading their résumé. The 'will' you have to learn from the interview."

3.14 Tips for Interviewing for a Job

I've interviewed for a position myself, assisted others, and acted as the hiring manager. What I feel most often is that the people who do best have prepared and thought through every aspect of the role and their offerings before walking into the room. While it's important to be yourself, it's also important to spend some time cultivating a winning attitude and understanding the interviewer's needs and concerns.

Below are tips to keep in mind for effective interviewing:

1) **Discover the Right Fit:** Remember you are interviewing them as much as they are interviewing you.

2) **Don't Be Desperate:** Employers don't want to know you want *any* job. They want to know why you want *this* job.

3) **Do Your Homework:** Learn about the company and the role. Ask yourself why you want to work there. Be prepared to articulate this.

4) **Be Prepared with Questions:** When I interviewed candidates, I often reserved the last ten or fifteen minutes of a thirty- or sixty-minute interview, respectively, for the candidate's questions. Their questions told me a lot about their preparation and motivation for interviewing.

5) **Sell Yourself:** Put your best foot forward in the limited amount of time you have.

6) **Tailor the Interview:** Different interviewers will care about different aspects of you. Share your stories and ask questions as they relate to the role of the person interviewing you. Are they the HR manager, hiring sales manager, potential peer, CEO? Adapt your message and questions to fit what they would care about and know. For example, when being interviewed by a sales manager, share illustrations on how you'll improve sales.

7) **Tailor Questions:** If the interviewer doesn't ask if you have questions, politely ask them near the end, "Would you mind if I ask some questions?" Ask appropriately, depending on the role of the individual you're speaking with. For the hiring manager, I would ask, "If I came on board, in a year from now, how would you measure my success as a hire?"

8) **Salary Requirements:** If you're asked about your salary requirements, I recommend holding off until they make you an offer unless you have a genuine concern about pay levels. You may say, "I would expect my compensation to be in line with the responsibilities of the position. I'd be happy to discuss further if we de-

termine we're a fit for each other." This usually stops that line of questioning and can save you thousands of dollars. See below for how to negotiate a higher salary.

9) **Thank the Interviewer:** At the end of the interview, thank the interviewer for their time and the opportunity to interview. If you have decided you would like to learn more, say so. Then ask about the next step. These questions are both powerful and too often unspoken. Say something like, "<Hiring Manager>, I have enjoyed this interview and I believe I would be a good fit in the role of _____ and able to add value to <Company>. What is the next step?" When they respond, ask, "When should I expect to hear from you?"

10) **Send Thank You Notes:** Mail a hand-written thank you note to each person you interviewed with. This stands out.

11) **Follow Up:** You've been given a timeline for when you can follow up. If you haven't heard from them by the date they said, don't worry. This will likely happen even if they're interested in you. Simply send a follow-up email thanking them for their time and for the opportunity. You can remind them of a point or two as to why you believe you'd be a good fit and ask when you may expect to hear from them. This will signal to your future employer that you're genuinely interested, responsible, and professional — all the qualities they'll be looking for.

3.15 Instructions — How to Negotiate a Higher Salary

*"Careers, like rockets, don't always take off on schedule.
The key is to keep working the engines."*
— Gary Sinise

It's always better to be working and find a better opportunity than to be sitting on the sidelines waiting for your mythical ideal job.

Companies have a range in mind for starting pay. This is negotiable. The more you are perceived to be valuable, the more the company is willing to offer the higher end of its range.

I experienced this firsthand when I was changing positions. I knew this would be the only time I would have a chance to negotiate.

After receiving the initial salary offer, I thanked my future boss for the offer. "Thank you for the offer. Can I talk to you about the salary?"

"Yes, of course," he replied.

"If I stay where I am, I'm due to receive bonuses that will take me to $\_\_\_\_\_$. For the past two years, I've had a goal to earn $\_\_\_\_$. Regardless of what the compensation is, if I come onboard, I'm going to be putting in my full effort. However, once there, I expect it's very difficult to earn more than 4.5 percent merit increases. Is there any chance you could do more to start me closer to my goal?"

His response: "You've done your homework, which is good and demonstrated why we want you." They boosted the offer $10,000 because I asked! This is the level on which all my future compensation was based.

Here are some steps to take if you're ready to ask for more money:

1) Determine what you want.
2) Find third-party reasons that justify the money you desire to be paid.
3) Be prepared to articulate the value you'll bring.

Use a Gratitude Sandwich to request more than you have been offered:

1) "Thank you for the offer."
2) "Based on market data, to be compensated fairly I would be paid between X and Y."
3) "I want to get to a number we can collaboratively agree upon."

Remember, no matter what number you finally accept, work hard to create more value than you are paid.

★ ★ ★

The right attitude can change your focus and the direction of your life. With your willingness to put in the self-discipline required and persist until you eventually reach your desired goal, you will achieve it. Keep this in mind as you encounter obstacles along the way. This will carry you quite far in your professional career as well.

In the next chapter, we'll talk about how to apply your successful attitude by managing your most valuable resource – your time.

Take Action

- ☐ Resolve to make work your friend; put your best effort into it.
- ☐ Make and follow a morning routine.
- ☐ If you need a pick-me-up, look yourself in the mirror and scream, "GOYA!"
- ☐ Pour your work into your ONE Thing. Make continual progress toward your 10,000 hours of mastery.
- ☐ Think through your needs, offerings, and attitude before entering an interview or salary negotiation.
- ☐ Identify someone you respect and admire. Invite them out to lunch. Ask their advice and follow it. Report back on what you did. Repeat. You now have a mentor!

Read These Books:

- ☐ *Who Moved My Cheese?* by Spencer Johnson
- ☐ *The Power of Positive Thinking* by Norman Vincent Peale
- ☐ *Success Through a Positive Mental Attitude* by Napoleon Hill and W. Clement Stone

4

VALUE YOUR TIME

"Dost thou love life? Then do not squander time, for that's the stuff life is made of."

Benjamin Franklin

Our time is the most precious gift we have, and it's the way we use our free time that determines our success. Often, people will lament not having enough time, but this is usually not true. We can always choose what actions we take in the limited free time we have. It all depends on how long or short our time horizon is for taking action. As Johann Wolfgang von Goethe wrote, "One always has time enough if one will apply it well."

I've found the problem of what to do will always arise if I don't know what I want. The cure for this is to know what I both want and need to accomplish over that given time frame. For example, for me to plan out a book-writing project over several months is a much different planning horizon than flying into a city, traveling to a hotel, and meeting up with a team to refine and practice a customer presentation the night before a meeting. One is planned in increments of days, while the other is planned in precious ten-minute blocks.

I find when I make plans based on a realistic assessment of the time necessary to perform the tasks, the scheduling becomes a bit of a puzzle. I may not always be able to perform the work at the level I would like, but I've often been pleasantly surprised to find that a slightly lower quality level was sufficient for tasks of lower importance.

4.1 Get Started

Aim toward your goals. Determine the steps to take. Then take them. Remember that you are not paid for your time. You are paid for the *value* you provide in the time you work. Aim to provide more value.

People often get caught up in thinking they don't know enough to begin. Instead, act with the knowledge you already have. More information will become known later at which time you can adjust. The key is to *get started!*

Time is more valuable than money. You always can get more money. But our time is finite. We just don't know our end date. Take action now!

I once woke up to the realization that if my start-up company didn't close at least one major project, our parent company would shut us down. This was a sobering realization. Would we secure a coveted project before the parent company pulled the plug? From then on, I felt it was a race against the clock. It was time to get started.

4.2 Make Time to Think

While your initial desire may get you moving, it's important to make time to think. This will help you best allocate your time to achieve what *you* want. Below are some of my favorite quotes on time and using your time to think:

- "Thinking is the hardest work there is, which is probably the reason why so few engage in it." — Henry Ford
- "If you fail to plan, you're planning to fail." — Anonymous
- "Most people fail in life because they major in the minor things." — Tony Robbins
- "You've got to think about big things while you're doing small things, so that all the small things go in the right direction." — Alvin Toffler
- "Self-discipline is the ability to do *what* you should do, *when* you should do it, *whether you feel like it or not*." — Elbert Hubbard
- "Concentrate. Put all your eggs in one basket — and then *watch that basket*." — Andrew Carnegie

4.3 Put Your Big Rocks in First

In his book *The 7 Habits of Highly Effective People*, Stephen Covey tells readers to put "First Things First." Imagine you have a large jar and three piles consisting of rocks, pebbles, and sand in front of you. If you first fill up the jar with the sand, you'll find yourself unable to put many of the big rocks in. However, if you first put in a select number of the big rocks, you'll still be able to pour in pebbles and finally sand. Your time is similar. In this analogy, the big rocks represent the most important things in your life — family, health, important work projects, and so on. The pebbles have less importance, and the sand has even lower importance. The point of the exercise is *not* to see how much you can fit in. The point is you will always have to choose *not* to do something. *You can't fit it all in!* However, you *can* fit in the most important things in your life. You *can* fit in your Big Rocks if you consciously choose to put them in first.

This is hard to live by. Small pebbles and sand are items that we can do daily and may be fun and easy like watching TV, surfing the internet, or checking social media. The Big Rocks may be taking a class, writing a book, or creating a business website. These Big Rocks may be contributing to your long-term goals. It's easy to fill your Jar of Time with small, meaningless activities. However, life is about choices. You can choose to do goal-achieving or tension-relieving activities. The former are difficult initially but pleasant later. The second are easy initially but hard to live with later. Summed up:

Easy choices → Hard life
Hard choices → Easy life
Which do you choose?

4.4 Focus on One Thing

The reason most major goals are not achieved is that we spend our time doing unimportant things first. The result of this tendency is that we find ourselves worn out and not much closer to our goals. The *immediate* is often the enemy of the *ultimate*. We tend to value the immediate more when we make decisions regarding our time and money. The truth is that a more successful and rewarding approach is to take the long view in order to determine the best course of action.

Apply the 80/20 Principle

Italian economist Vilfredo Pareto observed that wealth was unequally split in his country. The Pareto Principle — also known as the 80/20 Principle — states that 80 percent of the results of an undertaking are derived from 20 percent of the activities. For example, 80 percent of sales results are often generated by 20 percent of the sales force. And 80 percent of complaints come from 20 percent of customers. In some cases, the numbers may be 70/30 or 90/10. The idea isn't about the specific percentages, but about the recognition that all activities or contributors do *not* bring equal value. The key is to identify the vital few from the trivial many. Then focus on those activities or people who are creating the disproportionately large amount of value.

One of the highest-value activities a person can engage in is planning the use of their time. Time management expert Brian Tracy estimates that for every minute spent planning, you'll save ten minutes in execution. I've found this to be true. In addition to saving time, planning helps to orient your limited availability on the most important activities. Without this investment, it's easy to find yourself at the end of a day, week, month, or year wondering where the time went and if you have anything to show for it.

Identify Your ONE Thing

In his book *The ONE Thing,* Gary Keller advises that at the beginning of an undertaking, you should ask yourself the following question: "What is the ONE thing such that by doing it, everything else will be either easier or unnecessary?"

It can be helpful to add in qualifiers such as. "What is the ONE thing I can do in <A TIME FRAME> that will help me to achieve <GOAL>, such that by doing it, everything else is easier or unnecessary?"

For example, when I did this exercise, I asked myself, "What is the ONE thing I can do **this week** that will help me to accomplish **my goal of being a published author,** such that by doing it, everything else is easier or unnecessary?" My answer: "Edit one chapter a day for five days this week."

The discipline to ask this question at the beginning of the day and then continue to focus on that one action until it's complete will allow you to sail through the rough tides of inaction and indecision around you to make your goal a reality.

Oftentimes this may be an income or career goal. I asked myself, "What is the ONE Thing I could do to order to increase my income?" My answer was: "Increase sales." Then I asked, "What is the ONE Thing I could do to increase my sales?" My answer: "Concentrated effort and massive action to close one large project." This clarity allowed me to say no to all the other competing demands on my time and go all-out on a few projects that would have a large return.

4.5 Take Your Goal in Small Steps

Once you decide on a goal, break it down into incrementally smaller steps until you're down to steps that can be completed in one hour or less.

Break Down Your Book Reading Goal

I once heard that if you read one hundred books in a year, you could dramatically change your life. I undertook that challenge. I broke it down into determining I needed to read on average two books a week for fifty weeks. I created a spreadsheet to visually help me see it. When I selected a book, I broke down the goal further. I'd flip through the book to determine if it was worth investing the time to read. If so, I learned how it was structured and how I'd want to break up the reading process. How many pages? How many chapters? How many of each might this break down into per day if I'd want to read the book over seven days? How about faster? Slower?

Then, on a Post-it note, I wrote down my plan, listing the days of the week and dates I would read and how many pages or chapters I expected to read that day.

Would this work for you? Try it. It doesn't take but five to ten minutes. Now you have a track to run on for reading the book. It will help let you know if you're on or off pace. This helped me read more books in a four-month period than I previously had in a year!

Concentrate Your Energy

Part of the reason planning your time and focusing on one thing works is it allows you to concentrate your energy. This is nothing new; every culture and industry leader has similar advice.

- A Russian proverb says, "If you chase two rabbits you will not catch either one of them."
- Og Mandino, author of *The Greatest Salesman in the World,* says, "It is those who concentrate on but one thing at a time who advance in this world."
- General George S. Patton, who led the U.S. Army during World War II, had his entire career and success defined by this approach. He said, "You must be single-minded. Drive for the one thing on which you have decided."
- Legendary football coach Vince Lombardi, who won the first two Super Bowls and for whom the Super Bowl trophy is named, said, "Success demands singleness of purpose."
- Even thousands of years ago, this philosophy of concentrating efforts was advocated as well as the dangers of dissipating your efforts. Publilius Syrus said, "To do two things at once is to do neither."
- Finally, even in the Bible, in Luke 10:41–42, we find, "You are worried and distracted by so many things, but only one thing is necessary."

This is certainly timeless wisdom, however, there was a time when I chased after every new lead equally. Every company initiative rolled out I attempted to dutifully follow. Then I learned I was ultimately responsible for choosing what to focus on and to not dissipate my energies chasing too many rabbits at one time.

So don't worry about all the things facing you. Choose the one thing you can do that will make the biggest impact on your life right now, such that all other things would be easier and unnecessary. Then do it!

4.6 Instructions — Write Down Your Daily Activities

Once again, the problem of what to do will always arise if you don't know what you want. Each day, it's easy to become distracted. There are video games to play, iPads to view, YouTube videos to watch, and lots of other items competing for our attention. So, what do you do? Decide in advance what to do. This is the approach I've found to be very helpful for me in my work in sales. It can apply in any area where you have some control over how you will invest your time.

1) At the beginning of the day, make a list of everything you need to do for that day. Don't do this in your head. Write it down.

2) At the top of the piece of paper, write down the date. For the first activity write, "Plan Day." Once you have completed your planning, you'll be able to cross this off! This starts your day off with positive momentum!

3) Write down all the other items you can think of that are on your mind for accomplishing that day. This simply helps to get things out of your head. By putting them on a list you will feel reassured that there isn't something you're forgetting.

4) Now, you'll prioritize the list. You'll do this by putting a number in front of each activity. The goal is *not* to accomplish everything. Your goal is to make sure you're accomplishing the *most important* activities and then being comfortable choosing *not* to do the rest of your items in the time you have allocated.

5) Look over your list and determine your one thing. Give this a number 2 following your "Plan Day."

6) I've found it helpful to have a usual routine of items to start the day. For example, I've found that reading spiritual or mental texts and doing physical exercise helps me start my day off well.

7) Continue to look over the rest of your list identifying your Big Rocks and prioritizing them ahead of the smaller tasks.

8) This next step is one of the ones I've found different and most helpful. Once you've prioritized your list, go back, and on the right-

hand side, estimate how long in minutes you expect the activity to take. Write down when you expect to finish the activity. I've found this step alone is what has enabled my actions to have a sense of urgency and realism to become a reality. For example, if you give yourself twenty minutes to read, then do it. Then stop and move on to the next activity. I've found this oftentimes points out that I don't have enough time to complete many of the activities I want to complete. As a result, I realize I need to be more efficient in order to not go beyond the time I've allocated for myself to do a task.

9) While you won't be perfect, it helps you to not waste time and to get started and to work efficiently at the task during the time you have allocated to it. This happens because you know you have several other items you want to get done.

10) One of the keys is to give yourself enough time. Double the time you think you need to accomplish a creative task. You don't want to be rushed. This will allow you freedom to work diligently.

11) Once you've written down your plan for the day, compare it to your calendar to make sure you're scheduling around any preexisting appointments or commitments.

12) Now execute your day!

Endorphins are released by crossing off items on a list. You'll find motivation by accomplishing what you said you would. You'll also build up self-confidence and self-trust in your own abilities as you strengthen your muscle of accomplishing what you decided you would. The other great thing is that you're working on your most important tasks. You won't feel as though you worked frantically with nothing to show for it. Instead, just as a brick mason lays the foundation for a house one selected brick upon another, you will be building your career and life success one productive day at a time.

This approach brings peace of mind from having a track to run on. With purpose, it provides clarity about what direction we should move in.

Like a muscle, the more you exercise your ability to control your day, the more control you will gain over your day. Start by planning your weekend activities using the above approach. You'll find that by doing so, you may soon grow to where you find yourself in more control of your weekdays as well.

4.7 Schedule Your Weekly Goals

Nothing happens without a deadline. Whenever you write out a goal, make sure you write your deadline to accomplish it. Look at a calendar. Are you providing yourself a reasonable amount of time to accomplish your goal? Think about your other commitments. How much time will this goal take as you break it down into weekly and daily activities?

I've found it's hard to maintain momentum if you aren't acting upon your goal at least once each week. For this reason, break your large goal down into an increment that can be performed over the course of a week. For example, a goal to run a marathon may be broken down into: "Run three times a week for a total of ten miles." These become easy to plan and schedule.

This also fits with our natural way of creating habits. In *Atomic Habits*, author James Clear explains that habit formation requires four steps. I'll give examples related to running and wealth creation.

HABIT FORMATION STEP	HABIT OF RUNNING	HABIT OF WEALTH-BUILDING
Make It **Obvious**	Keep a public training record	Track your net worth
Make It **Attractive**	Picture a healthy and fit you	Picture yourself wealthy
Make It **Easy**	Run five minutes to start	Set up automatic withdrawals
Make It **Rewarding**	Bask in afterglow once finished	Celebrate milestones

4.8 Invest in Your Education

I believe one of the best investments you can make is to set a goal of increasing your education. This takes time but can yield substantial rewards. Benjamin Franklin famously said, "An investment in knowledge pays the best interest."

I do this by adopting the habit of daily reading. A favorite educator of mine and a pioneer for personal development is Jim Rohn. Below are a couple of my favorite phrases of his on the importance of reading:

- *"Miss a meal if you have to, but don't miss a book."*
- *"It isn't what the book costs, it is what it will cost you if you don't read it."*

My reading bounces around to various topics that I'm interested in. Certainly, I learn the subject of what I'm reading. But more than how much I'm reading, I feel simply engaging in the act of reading each day — even if only for five minutes — conditions my mind to be receptive.

Education is important, and so is staying sharp. Stephen Covey first popularized the phrase "Sharpening the Saw," to represent honing our physical and intellectual skills to stay sharp. However, the concept was popular long before. As the saying goes, "If I had five minutes to chop down a tree, I'd spend the first two-and-a-half minutes sharpening my ax."

If you aren't already, I recommend you set a daily habit to read for ten minutes each day from a book in a subject that interests you. It will change your life.

4.9 Take Time for Solitude

"To do much clear thinking a man must arrange for regular periods of solitude when he can concentrate and indulge his imagination without distraction."
— *Thomas Edison*

Ask someone how they're doing and very often you'll hear the response, "Busy!" This is said almost as a badge of honor. Push away from the busyness of life, invest in yourself, and don't mistake solitude for inaction. This quiet, reflective time may be the most productive activity you can engage in at that moment.

When I moved into a management role, a friend of mine cautioned me, "Mark, your time will no longer be your own. You will be at the mercy of those around you."

He was right. When you're in management, there are many demands on your time as you look to support the requests of people on your team, senior leaders, and peer managers while also seeking to advance your own ideas and initiatives.

For example, I regularly found myself involved in conference call sprints of thirty to sixty minutes that filled up entire eight-hour days with perhaps as little as thirty minutes unscheduled. One way for me to handle that pace was to carve out time for solitude.

When I've felt stressed, anxious, or overwhelmed, I found that taking ten to fifteen minutes to shut myself off from all the distractions of the world in favor of solitude works wonders. In an office environment, I've often moved into a conference room, turned off my phone, and shut down my email. In this environment I'm able to clear my head from the pressures of immediacy and identify what's important and those associated actions.

In a world where we are expected to be available all the time, it can be an unconscious energy drain. Unplugging from any inputs allows you take a step back to see the big picture and chart your course of action.

To help him collect his thoughts, Dwight D. Eisenhower would write memos to himself. The quiet reflection time was vital in helping him before issuing the command for the World War II D-Day invasion by American troops. It serves as a powerful reminder that even in the midst of an active war, it's critical to take time to be in silence and think.

DAD'S LITTLE BOOK OF WISDOM

4.10 Invest Your Time Until You Succeed

Have you ever felt that you're working hard but aren't getting any closer to your goals? You may be tempted to give up. Don't! If your plans are solid and you're going in the right direction, you may just need to keep at it longer.

That's the situation I found myself in at the end of my first seven months following my return to my first employer. I felt no closer to securing my first sale. I had to keep persevering and putting in the time and effort. My faith was the final ingredient that ultimately led to a stratospheric success. I'll tell the full story in Chapter 9.

4.11 Stick to It

In W. Clement Stone's book *Success Through a Positive Mental Attitude,* he shares what has become a mantra for me, "Where there is nothing to lose by trying and everything to gain if successful, by all means try. Do it now!"

And, once you reach your goal, don't relax too much. You may have built up significant momentum that can carry you to even greater heights.

Once I was fortunate enough to secure $10 million in new business in ten days! I wrote a thank-you email to my team and recounted the genesis of the deal:

On the afternoon of Thursday, June 13th, my VP called my boss to ask if there was any way we could accelerate the Water Meter project from an October booking to a June booking. When my boss asked me, my initial reaction was, "That's nuts!" My second reaction was, "What have we got to lose? Let's try!" We called and asked. The rest is history.

This was only possible because of the tremendous work we had done up to this point. We had developed a strong working relationship with the entire client's team for previous work. This had put us in the position to have the opportunity in the first place. However, the speed at which we were being asked to develop this was almost universally believed to be impossible.

I thought it was impossible too, but then a glimmer of hope entered the picture. I thought the worst case scenario was we'd fail doing everything in our power. I could live with that. Since we had nothing to lose but our time and and nothing to risk but looking foolish, I felt we might as well try. I give my company leaders credit: had they not asked we would have never attempted it. And after asking, they provided the support we needed. This along with similar-minded people whom I work with who were willing to put in massive work with a strong possibility of failure — it was likely that we'd fail yet we stuck to doing what we could anyway — that's what made this work.

4.12 Get "Unstuck"

As we progress, we all get stuck and bogged down. When that happens, don't throw in the towel and stop. Instead, resolve to get unstuck by continuing to move! Figure out your next action regardless of how small, and then do it! Examples may include reading, running, writing an email, making a phone call, or even hopping in a car for a ride. Do what it takes to generate the action and momentum needed to get unstuck.

At one point, I didn't have any sales prospects. I decided I would fill up my calendar and go to a number of places the following week. I created an appointment in a city four hours away. I informed my local branch office that I would be there over a two-day period and asked about availability. I sent emails out to a few potential clients asking for their availability on those days. Then, I called to follow up by scheduling appointment times. I ended up with four to five appointments because I planned in advance. I was specific and took action. This momentum helped spark more positive actions in the marketplace.

Another way I get myself unstuck is by becoming more granular in activities I could do. There are days I just don't have much energy. Rather than packing it in, I pick smaller rocks that aren't as overwhelming. I order these in ten- and fifteen-minute blocks. By making your tasks easier to check off, you'll create momentum. Check off items as you finish, and release those endorphins!

By accomplishing these smaller rocks, I gain momentum when I don't initially have the energy for tackling larger rocks. Oftentimes, by starting small on those days, I build emotional momentum and am then willing to take on a big rock.

4.13 Maintain Consistency

Routine brings results. An average person with a modest routine of daily self-improvement will outperform a disorganized genius ninety-nine times out of a hundred. Success in life is like riding a bicycle — you need to keep moving to stay balanced. Simple acts repeated may yield tremendous results over time. Examples of what have worked for me include reading, journaling, and making daily to-do lists, then staying focused on executing the most important items.

Jerry Seinfeld explained how he was able to achieve the feat of becoming a famous comedian. He did so by making a habit of writing a joke *every* day. He had a calendar by his bed. Every day when he would go to bed, he would put a large red "X" across the day if he had successfully written a joke. Not every joke he wrote was particularly funny, but enough of them were. His goal was to not break the streak. He developed his joke-writing muscle and discipline by making it a daily habit.

4.14 Control What You Can Control

"The best time to plant a tree is twenty years ago.
The second-best time is today."
— Chinese Proverb

Resolve today to take 100 percent responsibility for everything that you are and everything you become. Never complain. Never explain. A successful attitude is one in which you retain the locus of control instead of worrying about the past. The past is set in stone, the future has yet to be written, and only in the present can we act.

Motivational speaker Denis Waitley asserts, "Happy people plan actions. They don't plan results." Focus your energy. Control what you can control because the road to hell is paved with good intentions. It isn't about what you *intend* to do, it's about what you *actually* do!

4.15 Calculate Your Hourly Rate

What is your hourly rate? When you go to work as a doctor, a business person, a factory worker, or at McDonald's, you're trading your time and life energy for money. How do you know that it's a good trade?

At my first job, when I was seventeen years old, I earned the minimum wage of $4.25 an hour working at Little Caesars Pizza. I had no unique skills and was easily replaceable. In fact, I really wasn't even that good at it — I was too methodical and slow. I diligently attempted to put all the toppings on the pizza according to the pictures that hung above the pizza-making stations while others were frantically tossing them on and churning them out much faster than I did. When large orders came in, which do you think the manager preferred — slow and methodical or fast and "good enough"? Yep — not me!

After I earned my engineering degree, my hourly rate went up to $19.25 an hour, or 4.5 times what I initially earned. Why? I had invested four years at college learning engineering skills that I could then utilize to help my employer generate revenue. I was more valuable to my employer and as a result they were willing to pay me more.

What are you being paid per hour? Calculate this by adding up the income you're paid in a year. Then divide by the number of hours you worked that year. A traditional employee may work a forty-hour job with two weeks of vacation. If this is your situation, divide your income by 2,000 hours. This is your hourly rate. For example, if you earn $60,000 in a year, your hourly rate is $30 an hour ($60,000/2,000 hours).

Track your hourly rate so you can see your progress and also determine what tasks to perform or not.

However, it's a trap to think you should be paid this hourly rate regardless of what you're doing during your time. This is the surest way to ultimately lose your job or your clients. Instead, aim to always create more value for your employer or client than you are being paid for.

When you do this consistently, you'll become more valuable to the marketplace and it will drive your income up. If not with your current employer, then another will be happy to pay you more.

4.16 When Not to Invest Your Time

Now that you're educated about your hourly rate, when should you choose not to do a task? Whenever you can, hire someone to perform it at a rate that's lower than yours. This will reserve more of your time for higher-value tasks.

Also, if you're stressed and anxious about a task or activity, see if you can identify someone else who may be better suited. What may take you hours may be done by someone else in less time and with higher quality. If you need others to do something, ask! you're then multiplying your time by having others do it.

For me, this is why I stopped attempting to do any plumbing work. It would take me hours, I never enjoyed it, and oftentimes I would feel frustrated at the end. I have always found it a much better use of time and money to hire someone else who is more specialized, thereby allowing myself to put my energy into either my family, rest, or my own profession.

The only difference between Warren Buffett, your CEO, and you is how you have used your time up until this point. Now the question is, "How will you use it going forward?"

★ ★ ★

Time is our most precious gift, and how we use it determines our rewards in life. We often trade our time and life energy for money, so in the next chapter we'll discuss how to best manage those financial resources.

Take Action

- ☐ Build a daily morning routine. Include at least ten minutes of reading.
- ☐ Prioritize your goals, then pick one to work on first.
- ☐ Track your progress in a journal.
- ☐ Take time to think, learn, and be alone.
- ☐ Calculate your hourly rate.
- ☐ Think through how you can give your employer or clients more in value than you're currently being paid.
- ☐ Delegate tasks as necessary to invest toward better uses of your time.

Read These Books:

- ☐ *The 7 Habits of Highly Effective People* by Stephen R. Covey
- ☐ *Eat that Frog!* Brian Tracy
- ☐ *Getting Things Done* by David Allen

5

MANAGE YOUR FINANCES

"Expenses rise to meet income."

Parkinson's Law

Even though money determines many of our decisions, most people don't take time to plan out their finances, understand their financial goals, or practice healthy money habits. Money, contrary to popular belief, is not the root of all evil. Love of money above all else, however, will quickly encourage bad behavior. In this chapter, I'll cover some easy and highly effective budgeting and money management practices. These will ensure you're on your way to financial independence and healthy money habits no matter what your bank account balance is today.

5.1 Develop a Long-Time Perspective

After reading *The Millionaire Next Door* by Thomas J. Stanley and William D. Danko, I looked around me and realized I was chasing the trappings of success, which required an ever-greater amount of income to sustain. The book helped me to adopt a long-time perspective and realize how much interest I was paying on student loans, car loans, and mortgages. Once you do a similar exercise and look at how much your total cost will be, I'm confident you'll avoid paying the exorbitant credit card fees and interest rates if you maintain a balance.

It's wise to avoid the furniture and electronic product offers to finance purchases. Financing costs can make a purchase significantly more expensive. Better to wait and save up to purchase with cash. You will have more options, you will pay less in the long run, and you won't have the increased interest costs.

According to the follow-up book, *The Next Millionaire Next Door* by Thomas J. Stanley and his daughter Sarah Stanley Fallaw, the single most important trait of surveyed millionaires when it comes to success is, "Being well disciplined." Discipline, in this sense, is the ability to delay gratification; to do the hard and necessary work today to enjoy the fruits later on. It's taking the slow and steady approach of the tortoise rather than expecting riches to come quickly like the hare.

If you wish to be wealthy, seek to be paid interest and avoid paying it.

As management guru Peter Drucker says, "We greatly overestimate what we can accomplish in one year. But we greatly underestimate what we can accomplish in five years." Only in the past few years, have I set five-year plans. The focus beyond a first year allowed me to not be discouraged if seeds I planted didn't yield results right away. It's like the bamboo tree that grows underground for four years before sprouting up to amazing heights in the fifth year.

How do you do amazing things? Follow St. Francis of Assisi's advice, "First do what is necessary, then do what is possible, and before long you will find yourself doing the impossible."

Like planting, watering, and nurturing your bamboo, give your financial goals the same careful attention. Take it one step at a time. If you do, you'll reap uncommon results. As the saying goes, "Yard by yard, it's hard. Inch by inch, anything's a cinch."

5.2 Adopt a Healthy Attitude about Money

I used to be embarrassed about wanting to earn money and accumulate financial security. I'm not sure why it's such a taboo subject. But I believed the subject of money was like religion, politics, or sex — never to be discussed in polite company. It seemed dark and mysterious. With these conflicting beliefs, it was unsurprisingly difficult for me to accept attracting money into my life. I'm glad podcasts like *ChooseFI* and *Millionaires Unveiled* are discussing finances and wealth accumulation out in the open and removing the stigma. Life is much less stressful when you don't have to worry about your next paycheck or how you're going to cover an unplanned expense.

Have you ever examined your attitudes about money? Wealth is a state of mind. So is poverty. Broke is a temporary condition. A financial condition is not static. Your beliefs and attitudes about yourself, your abilities, and about money, will determine what you later receive.

You can make money, or you can make excuses, but not both. Money is not everything. The major value in life is not what you *get*, but what you *become*. In 2 Peter 2:19, we find that "a person is a slave to whatever overcomes him." The more you grow, the more you can tackle problems and not be overcome by them.

U.K. Prime Minister Winston Churchill said, "We make a living by what we get, but we make a life by what we give." Some of the world's biggest fortunes were accumulated by those who were focused on giving and creating along their journey.

5.3 Give like the Good Samaritan

You may hear people say that money is the root of all evil, but they're mistaken. The Bible states, "The *love of* money is the root of all evil." Placing anything in our hearts above God is evil. Jesus tells us we should love the Lord God with all our heart. This is the first and greatest commandment.

Jesus tells the parable of the Good Samaritan in the Gospel of Luke. It's about a traveler who is attacked by robbers, beaten, stripped of his clothes, and left half-dead on the road. First, a priest and then a Levite come along the road, but they ignore the man in need. Finally, a Samaritan comes upon him and is moved with compassion. Samaritans and Jews despised each other, but the Samaritan felt moved to help the injured man. After pouring wine over his wounds and bandaging him, he takes him to an inn for care. He takes out two silver coins and gives them to the innkeeper with the instruction, "Take care of him. If you spend more than what I have given you, I shall repay you on my way back."

I have often thought of the Good Samaritan parable and realized Jesus illustrated how money can be used for His purpose. If the Good Samaritan had not had any money, he wouldn't have been able to pay for the traveler's care. Money is not evil. It's a tool to be used well by the one who wields it.

I like to view the holding of money like a trustee. Ultimately, everything we have has been given to us by God. At the end of our days, we will be held accountable according to what good we were able to accomplish with what was given to us. When you keep this in mind, you'll make better choices.

In Hebrews 13:5, we find, "Let your life be free from love of money but be confident with what you have, for he has said, 'I will never forsake or abandon you.'" Be careful to avoid the trap of consumerism. Do you really need a larger house with rooms that will be unoccupied 90 percent of the time? Do you need a new car every two years? Do you feel you need to update your wardrobe to keep up with fashion? If you want these things because you'll enjoy them — great, enjoy! But realize we are marketed to almost continuously. Resist. Don't let yourself be swept away by someone else's idea of what you should buy. Keeping up with the Joneses is a never-ending battle. Find what brings you joy for both yourself and the good you can do around you. Remember that a *man who owns little, is little owned.*

5.4 Be a Producer

> *"We have no more right to consume happiness*
> *without producing it than to consume wealth*
> *without producing it."*
> *— George Bernard Shaw*

Imagine you plop down on the coach, grab the remote, and turn on the TV. On comes your favorite Food Network show, a recent Disney movie, or perhaps the evening news. You're consuming the media that has been created for viewers like you. While you're watching, you're exposed to commercials to help pay for the creation of this content.

There are two sides to this equation. Producers actively create the content, products, and experiences while consumers passively take in the content, products, and experiences. We're all consumers at many times in our life. Nothing wrong with that — our economy needs consumers. The trap comes when we're not mindful of which role we play — and spend too much time as a consumer. At times, intentionally choose to be a producer. You'll be happiest while you're making your greatest contribution to the world around you. This occurs when you're most fully utilizing the talents and abilities you've been given and contributing to society.

The marketplace will also reward you for being a producer. It pays you according to the value you create for the marketplace. Are we all equal in the eyes of the Lord? Yes, of course! However, not in the eyes of the marketplace. If you want to be paid more, then create more value for the marketplace. *The more you pour out, the more life will be able to pour in.*

5.5 Learn to Save

John D. Rockefeller, who was perhaps the richest man alive when he lived, had four tips he taught his children for allocating their income. Let this timeless financial advice guide you.

1. Give the first 10 percent of all you earn to charity.
2. Save 10 percent of all you earn.
3. Pay 10 to 20 percent down on your debts.
4. Live on your remaining 60 to 70 percent.

A similar response came out of a survey conducted of over 10,000 millionaires.[3] They were each asked, "What is the number one habit a person has to adopt in order to become a millionaire?" The most common response was simple: "Spend less than you earn." It's clear that frugality wins. Frugality and saving, of course.

When I started at my first employer, fresh out of college, my first

3 Go to www.Dadslittlebookofwisdom.com
to access links to more millionaire interviews and insights.

manager sat me down and said to me, "Mark, if you learn to save 10 percent of your income now and invest it for forty years using compound interest, you'll be a multimillionaire." It inspired me to never invest less than 10 percent of my income. I still have the little yellow Post-it where he wrote those numbers! That was a great plan to get started. Over the past five years, my wife and I have gone from putting away 15 percent of our income to saving 50 percent of it. On the podcasts I listed it's common to hear stories of those saving 30 to 50 percent of their income, and even over 80 percent in some extreme examples. The *ChooseFI* book explains the mantra of spend less, save more, and invest better. Wherever you are, I implore you just begin the habit of paying yourself first, *now!*

When you do, you'll be able to put your money to work for you. To illustrate the impact of compound interest, I'll use an example modified from Burton Malkiel, author of *A Random Walk Down Wall Street* — but we'll use a twin sister and brother example. Let's call them Karen and David. The have both just turned sixty-five — the traditional retirement age. Karen opened a retirement account at age twenty and continued to invest $4,000 a year for the next twenty years. At forty, she decided to stop contributing additional funds, and simply let the money grow tax-free in a retirement account at 10 percent a year.

David didn't begin to invest until he turned forty, starting to invest just as Karen was ending her active contributions. Similarly, he invested the same $4,000 a year in a tax-free retirement account earning 10 percent, but plowing money in right up until he turned sixty-five for a total of twenty-five years of contributions.

When we compare contributions, Karen invested a total of $80,000, while David invested a total of $100,000. However, the difference is in *when* they invested. Karen started early. David started twenty years later. How much of a difference does that make? Amazingly it produces a *600 percent difference!*

Let's look at the math. Karen, who invested and stopped before her brother began, ends up with $2.5 million at retirement time when she hits age sixty-five. David, despite contributing $20,000 more than his sister, has less than $400,000 at age sixty-five. *That is a difference of over $2 million!* Be like Karen — invest early. Also, nudge your siblings to begin investing early so they can enjoy those vacations with you to Hawaii!

5.6 Instructions — How to Budget Expenses

I've used a budget for over twenty years. To get started, sometimes simple is best. The first one I used was a spreadsheet with the numbers 1-31 going down for each day and ten major categories along the top. I would record where the money went.

My ten categories are:

1) Charity
2) Savings
3) Taxes
4) Mortgage Payment or Rent
5) Household Misc.
6) Automobile Expenses
7) Food and Entertainment
8) Insurance
9) Personal Misc.
10) Business

I still use these broad categories with greater detail in subcategories. As you increase the number of expenditures and combine with a spouse and expenses for kids, you may want to use a financial program to help you track your income and expenditures. While my wife and I use Quicken, there are also other programs on the market such as Mint and Personal Capital.[4]

4 Go to www.Dadslittlebookofwisdom.com
   to download both simple budget tools.

For managing household budgets, it isn't the *large* expenditures but the *small* ones that will siphon off your wealth. Think of it as a bathtub full of water. If there are a bunch of small leaks in the bathtub, out flows your water. It's important to plug all those small leaks. Below are a few ideas on steps you can take:

1) Make a list of items you need to purchase prior to entering a store.
2) Buy on sale (but only items on your list).
3) Use coupons.
4) Exchange clothing with family and friends who have kids older and younger than yours.
5) Switch providers for TV, internet, phone, insurance, gas, electric, and propane, etc.

Intentional shopping can lead to spending less with little to no discernible difference in quality.

Remember the whole reason to budget is to aid you in your quest to spend less than you earn. You don't have to be rigid. If you try to be too rigid, you may give up maintaining a budget altogether. In fact, in all the time I've maintained a budget, I have yet to have a single month in which I didn't alter it from the beginning of the month to the end. We adapt. You'll need to as well. By tracking your expenses, you'll have insight into what expense you'll likely have and when you can allow freedom for more dinners out, the latest book, or how much to save each month to enjoy that guilt-free vacation trip to Disney World. In short, budgeting keeps things under control.

5.7 Pay Off Your Student Loans the Smart Way

When I was a junior at the University of Notre Dame, I recall overhearing a conversation that helped shape my financial life. It was between a graduating senior we'll call Matt and my roommate Randy.

Matt: I'm outta here! I'm excited to join the real world and begin working. I certainly have lots of student loans I need to repay.

Randy: Yeah, I hadn't thought of that before.

Matt: Well, fortunately, I have a plan to pay them off as fast as possible.

Randy: Really, what's your plan?

Matt: Simple. I'm going to organize them in order from smallest to largest. Then I'll pay any extra money I can toward the loan with the smallest amount until it is paid off. Then I'll roll the money I would have been paying on that loan to the next smallest until that one is paid off. Then I'll repeat.

Randy: Why don't you pay off the loan with the highest interest rate first?

Matt: That sounds like a good idea, but the loans with the highest interest rates are the ones with the largest balance. Paying those off will take much longer. I know myself. It would be hard to stay motivated for so long. I'd rather get some easier wins. This will help me stay motivated. By paying off even the smallest loan, the payments I have to make will be lower, so I'll have flexibility.

Randy: Good plan. I'll do that too!

My Thoughts: Yes, me too!

This is the plan I followed and it worked out great. Below is the cost breakdown of my four-year education:

Tuition: $80,000
Room and board: $20,000
Total: $100,000

My parents committed to helping pay for $20,000 of this. For the balance, I worked during the school year and was fortunate to pick up some scholarships after my freshman year. But most of the money was paid for by student loans.

I had eight student loans, two of which were in my parents' name because they wouldn't lend a student the full amount. These totaled $55,000.

I created a spreadsheet with several tabs to help me stay focused and be excited about paying down the debt. One of these was a chart showing the principal going down over time.[5] The phrase "Whatever you focus on grows" applies. I focused on how I could reduce that amount and it provided motivation for my job as a salesperson. When I was fortunate to land a larger project earning a larger commission, instead of going out and splurging on food or "stuff" that I wouldn't care about a month after purchasing, I put it toward paying off my loans.

I created a debt snowball. It started out slowly at first and then became bigger. After marrying my wife, we accelerated the repayment even faster with dual incomes. As a result, we paid off our loans early and saved over $17,000 in interest!

5.8 Instructions – The Debt Snowball

1) List all your outstanding debts, including student loans, credit cards, car loans, etc.

2) List the outstanding amounts, interest rates, monthly payments, and number of months you have left to pay them off.

3) Calculate your Loan's Total Life Cost. Multiply the monthly payment by the remaining number of months to pay off the loan. This is the total amount you will pay for the life of the loan from this point forward including principal and interest.

4) Calculate the Total Interest. This is the amount you will pay if you make only the regular payments. Start with the Loan's Total Life Cost and subtract the Current Loan Balance.

5) Put loans in order based on lowest current balance.

---

5 Go to www.Dadslittlebookofwisdom.com to
   download a Student Loan Reduction Chart.

6) Find any extra money you can and apply that to your loan. This is the beginning of your Debt Snowball.

7) As you apply your extra payments, they will lower your outstanding amount rapidly. Like a regular snowball, your Debt Snowball will pick up speed the more you increase it and as you pay off outstanding debts and roll those payments.

8) Calculate your new Total Payment, Total Interest, and Interest Savings.

Once you calculate your Total Interest, I'm willing to bet it will shock you. That's great! Let that serve to motivate you to take action. Pay a little extra each month to get your Debt Snowball bigger. Even if you have to start small — start! Skip the $5 coffee or $10 lunch out to apply some funds. Paying off your debts faster may save you tens of thousands in avoided interest!

5.9 Manage Credit with Care

Credit cards were introduced in the 1970s. Prior to the 1970s, people who didn't have the money simply had to go without or wait until they saved their funds. Once credit cards were introduced, people no longer had to wait. This resulted in a booming economy and a decline in self-discipline. Credit cards are very convenient for purchasing airline tickets, online shopping, gas, and so on.

However, many of these same benefits can be provided by a debit card. A debit card looks like a credit card with one big difference. A debit card is tied to your bank and allows you to spend only money that you have in your bank account. A credit card will allow you to borrow money you do not have with an obligation to pay it back, typically in monthly payments.

Credit cards carry outrageously high interest rates, such as 16 to 26 percent! To entice people to acquire and then spend on credit cards, companies spend millions (if not billions) on advertising with offers to provide points, cash back, or other perks. Be very careful.

For much of my adult life, I shunned the perks offered by credit card companies even though they were very enticing. I have been burned from a slip or two over twenty-plus years. Only after firmly developing the discipline to not overspend and pay off your credit card balances in full every month would I advise using a credit card.

Check out the ChooseFi.com website and podcast for a supportive financial community. Once you've honed your financial discipline, they also have travel rewards and credit card tips.

5.10 Dave Ramsey's 7 Baby Steps, Including Developing an Emergency Fund

In his best-selling book *The Total Money Makeover,* Dave Ramsey provides a simple formula for how to build wealth. The genius in his advice is in its simplicity.

Below are his 7 Baby Steps:

Baby Step 1 — $1,000 to start an Emergency Fund
Baby Step 2 — Pay off all debt using the Debt Snowball
Baby Step 3 — 3 to 6 months of expenses in savings
Baby Step 4 — Invest 15 percent of household income into Roth IRAs and pre-tax retirement
Baby Step 5 — College funding for children
Baby Step 6 — Pay off home early
Baby Step 7 — Build wealth and give!

The first and third of Dave Ramsey's Baby Steps are to develop and then fully fund an emergency fund. There are debates about how big this should be. Some say between three to six months of expenses and that this money should be kept very liquid, not subject to the fluctuations of the market. We decided that $20,000 in a very accessible savings account, in addition to our Roth IRAs that were accessible if we were in dire straits, provided us the security we needed to feel comfortable.

Later, we reduced our liquid cash and put more to work in a Roth IRA that we could access in an emergency.

You never know when your car may break down, one of your kids may end up in the hospital, or a sudden turn of events leaves you with reduced income or out of work entirely. Choose to build an emergency fund when you have the income. The most important value of an emergency fund is peace of mind. It's much easier to sleep at night when you have significant savings in the bank.

5.11 How *Not* to Buy a Car

My first car-buying experience proves that inexperience is costly, but not fatal. I did, however, learn a lot about negotiation and large purchases in general.

I needed a car to travel from South Bend, Indiana, to Chicago. I went to two or three car dealers. At the Toyota dealer, the salesperson told me I could lease a 1998 Toyota Corolla by just making the monthly payments. The advertised price of $199 a month soon ballooned as I was presented with various options that I kept accepting.

Salesman: "Would you want wood grain interior for only another $42/month?"
Mark: "Sure!"
Salesman: "Would you want the gold hubcap exterior for only another $35/month?"
Mark: "Cool! Yes!"

It went on until I was paying $310 a month, or 50 percent more than I expected! Had I realized I was being asked to spend an additional $4,000 [($310-$199) x 12 months x 3 years], I would have never agreed. But I didn't realize it.

Dave Ramsey would refer to this as a "Stupid Tax" — money I spent because I didn't understand financial math at the time.

My Stupid Tax was almost much greater. As this was a lease, I had purchased only 15,000 miles a year. At the end of my three-year lease, if I drove over the allotted 45,000 miles, I would owe a ridiculous amount per mile over my allocation. Fortunately, at that time, I was dating my future wife. She was working for BP. Since they wanted to test the impact of their gasoline on vehicles after wear and tear, they let employees drive company cars to test the fuel. My wife volunteered to drive one of the company cars. I drove her Saturn. We did this for over three months at the end of my term, saving thousands of extra mileage fees.

Be very careful with leases. In fact, I recommend avoiding them altogether.

The next time I purchased a car, I did much better, but I still made mistakes. I shopped around virtually by sending an email request to car dealers detailing the options I wanted for a Honda Civic. Only after I received quotes did I go visit the dealership offering the best combination of price and local service.

I felt so proud of myself walking into the dealership with my quote, knowing I had saved a few thousand dollars, that I relaxed and let myself purchase the extended warranty — which gave the dealer back all the money I saved!

Later I learned more about the math. According to Dave Ramsey, "On average, you'll pay about $1,500 on an extended warranty, and the average repair is $180. I don't recommend buying extended warranties, ever. If you can't afford a $200 repair on a car, then you can't afford the car."

I paid $1,800 for the extended warranty. I drove it for close to 200,000 miles and it never had a repair that qualified. To top it off, I financed the car purchase and the extended warranty, costing even more money. Learn from my mistakes. Don't buy extended warranties. Buy reliably manufactured cars and self-insure with a small amount of savings. Second, keep saving. By saving up to purchase something you can afford, you'll avoid all the interest payments.

5.12 How *to* Buy a Car

The next time I bought a car, I had a much better plan!

Being in sales, you might think that I like buying cars. I don't. The same emotions and fears that go through the minds of over 95 percent of car buyers go through mine. "Am I getting a good deal? Am I being taken advantage of? Can I believe them?" It also serves as a reminder to me of what type of sales professional I do and don't want to be. This is a classic transactional sale as opposed to a business or relationship sale. This is a one-time transaction that's fraught with games and gimmicks. Is it any surprise that most people don't relish the experience?

I want to give you insight to help you with your next major purchase. Below you'll find thirteen lessons I learned to aid you during your next car-buying experience. These same lessons aren't limited to car purchasing and can be applied to other major decisions such as buying a house, a major renovation, or higher education. The purchase may change — the psychology of interacting with other humans doesn't.

Lesson 1: Do your your research.

I went to the library and pulled *Consumer Reports* for the most reliable 2011, 2012 and 2013 cars. I was surprised to learn that in addition to the staple Camry and Accord ratings, Hyundai's Sonata was a top scorer and in some cases rated as a better value. I included Sonata[6] in my list to investigate.

Do your research. A little time comparing options will reap you a better end result.

Lesson 2: Let your emotions enter only after thinking straight.

Many big financial decisions are emotional. I went through websites such as Autotrader.com, Cars.com, and local dealer websites to search pre-owned inventory. I cast a wide net of possible options including models,

---

6 When you read this, the technology features and search methods may have changed — the practice of doing your research will not.

years, mileages, and car dealer locations. I put together a spreadsheet of all the cars I could find out there — hey, I'm an analytical engineer! Once I narrowed down the selection, it was like tightening a net.

Don't act on impulse. Gather your options and then return a day or two later with a clear head.

Lesson 3: Your trade-in is another negotiation. Find out its value up-front.
During the week and a half that led up to Black Friday, when I planned to buy my new car, I did my online research. That helped narrow down the search, but it left out an important part of my car-buying process — the value of my trade-in. I realized I could possibly get more money by selling it myself, but I didn't want to go through the hassle. Each dealer has a different view of the value of my car and it would have a significant bearing on what my net out-of-pocket expense would be. In addition to the local Toyota dealer, I visited a local Honda dealer and CarSense. The Honda dealer offered me $3,500 and CarSense offered $2,000.

You need to think through the whole buying game in advance. When you do, you'll be prepared. The money you save will be your proof.

Lesson 4: Different dealers have different business models.
CarSense offered the lowest trade-in value. They tout themselves as a "no haggle" place to buy a pre-owned car. And that seemed true — they probably would be an "easy place to buy." Their sales prices were reasonable, but with the low trade-in value they offered, it wasn't the best place for me. Modifying an old real estate adage, "They make their money when they buy and realize it when they sell."

Companies will gladly take as much of your money as you will allow them to take. Let them have someone else's. Do your homework.

Lesson 5: Car Games: Watch for an initial high trade-in offer to entice you to return.
My local Toyota salesperson offered me $5,000 to $6,000 for my car, so it was hard to find a better deal. Armed with the assessment of car

options and trade-in values, I was now ready to buy. I picked out my top car choices at the local Toyota dealer and planned to make my purchase.

There are lots of sales enticements in the form of low advertised offers to get you in the door. Be wary.

Lesson 6: Call ahead to confirm that the car you desire is still available before you arrive.

On Black Friday, I showed up at my local Toyota dealer a little after noon. When I got there, Todd greeted me. This was the third face-to-face interaction over a span of two weeks. We went back to look at his computer to find out what was still available. After I read off my top two choices from my spreadsheet, he replied, "I'm sorry, but it looks like we no longer have those two. But we can go out to the lot and show you what we still have available." I asked myself, "Is this true? Is this a bait and switch to cars I'm not as knowledgeable about? Is he trying to create fear that I'll miss out by not acting quickly?"

Before you invest your valuable time driving to a store, a car dealer, or meeting with someone, make a quick phone call. You may save yourself a trip.

Lesson 7: Car Games: Watch for a bait and switch.

We went out and looked at the available cars. Compared to my target cars, these were newer, higher-end, low-mileage cars with a higher asking price, all in the $18,000 to $19,000 range. I didn't want to play games, so I told him what I wanted. "I'm looking for a two- to three-year-old Camry I can buy for cash for no more than $10,000 after my trade-in. You said you could offer up to $6,000 for my car. I expect that would have worked for the original cars I was interested in. I'd be happy with any of these if you can make it work. If not, I understand."

He frowned and then replied, "Let's go back in, and let me talk with my sales manager."

After an appropriate time, the salesperson reemerged and announced, "Good news! It turns out the original car you wanted is available, just at another lot. We were taking it to be sold at an auction.

It will cost us $200 to bring it back, but we can make the deal work if that's what you want."

While I questioned why my originally desired car was suddenly now available, I didn't dwell on it because I knew this would be an excellent bargain. "Great," I said.

Caveat emptor — buyer beware!

Lesson 8: Car Games: Watch for last-minute changes.

Todd continued, "My sales manager just needs to confirm the condition of your car to make sure your car is worth the trade-in value."

As he took my Camry's keys and disappeared into the sales manager's office, my self-talk kicked in, "Mark, the deal is not done. Be prepared for changes. Is this their opportunity to switch the terms of the deal before it was finalized? Or will I get this great deal?"

Once Todd the salesperson returned, he went into relationship mode. He started chatting with me about family and Thanksgiving. I told myself, "He's trying to form a bond with me. He wants me to like him, so if something changes, I'll feel compelled to go forward with him."

Todd then disappeared into the sales manager's office for a long time. Upon his return he informed me, "Unfortunately, my sales manager said your car has been in accidents and isn't worth as much as he thought. We will only be able to offer $4,500 for your trade-in, which will bring the Camry you want down to $11,000." It was still an attractive deal, but not as attractive as I was led to believe. I was disappointed in their last-minute change to my appraised trade-in value.

Never forget your most valuable negotiating tactic as a buyer — your ability to walk away. If you don't like the deal, leave.

Lesson 9: Keep your options open.

I agreed to put down a deposit, but since he had informed me that the car wasn't on the lot and I couldn't see it, I requested that my deposit be fully refundable for any reason until Monday, when I would actually have a chance to see the car. If I couldn't do any better by then, I would go forward with the transaction.

Building on the advice above, if you have options, you will feel confident in asking for what you want. You'll know if they can't provide it, you can walk away.

Lesson 10: Remove "Sales Manager Car Games" by going to the top.

After investing two hours at the car dealer, I returned to my office not satisfied with how things had ended. So I did more research. I figured I already had a good deal on a Camry, but through my car shopping, I realized what I *really* wanted was a Sonata. I walked into the Hyundai dealership at 6:15 p.m. I asked to speak to the sales manager. The receptionist said he was busy. Since I persisted in speaking to a manager, she directed me to the general manager, Oliver.

Deal with the decision maker. This minimizes games.

Lesson 11: Talk straight.

As soon as I was in his office, I told him, "I've already put down a deposit to buy a Toyota Camry earlier today, but they started playing games. I'm here to see if you can provide what I want, and if so, I'll buy a car from you." I explained the trick was on the value for my trade-in. I told him, "My car was involved in two accidents, has 148,000 miles on it and the other dealer offered me $4,500."

He called his used car manager, Steve, into his office, introduced me, and took my keys to have my car appraised. Once Steve left, Oliver sat back behind his desk at his computer and said, "Now let's see if we have a car that you want." I had five cars that were on my list. I gave them to him in random order, and he confirmed one by one that each of them was still available. "It looks like you've got your pick of the lot!"

When you talk straight, oftentimes the other person will respect you and reciprocate by treating you the same way.

DAD'S LITTLE BOOK OF WISDOM

Lesson 12: Don't be afraid to walk away.

Then Oliver had one of his salesmen, Anton, take me for a test drive. After the test drive, Anton took me to a chair while he went to find out my trade-in value. When he returned, he showed me a paper with two possible Sonata options, both of them closer to $11,000 than $10,000 after the $4,200 they offered me for my trade-in. I promptly said, "Thank you," stood up, and shook his hand. He said, "Did you want to do something?" I said, "I told Oliver what I wanted to have happen and to find out if you could do it or not." Anton looked confused and said, "Here comes Oliver now, let's talk with him." Was this yet another game — being passed down to the salesperson with the sales manager watching in the wings? Oliver asked me what was going on.

I replied, "I appreciate you letting me know what you could do. I already told you what I needed, but it doesn't seem like it's possible. I won't waste your time any longer."

Oliver said, "Well, did you like the 2013? If we could do it for $10,000 before taxes and tags would you consider it?"

I replied, "I would buy it."

"Okay, let me see what we can do." A few minutes later Oliver returned, stating, "I'll lower the price to $14,200. With your trade-in that will bring you to your desired $10,000."

Be prepared to be tested. Yet, once again, exercising your powerful option of walking away will bring about the best possible deal you could get.

Lesson 13: Celebrate!

By 7:10 p.m. (less than an hour later), I was done with my car-buying negotiations. Ultimately, it felt like draft day and I got my number one pick. I bought the car I had ranked with the best value for which I felt I could pay cash. It was a great feeling!

Congratulations! If you've done most or all of these steps, you will have saved more of your hard-earned money during your next major purchase. You have a right to feel proud!

5.13 Invest in the Stock Market

Financial independence is like a three-legged stool resting on savings, insurance, and investments. One of my goals is to live off the income my investments generate. This is called financial independence and is certainly achievable.

In 2007, famed investor Warren Buffett bet a million dollars that an index fund would outperform a collection of hedge funds over the next ten years. In January 2018, he won that bet. That means that the best and brightest of Wall Street find it exceptionally difficult to consistently pick stocks that will beat the market.

In his February 2018 letter to shareholders, Buffett explained,

> "Making money on the stock market does not require great intelligence, a degree in economics, or a familiarity with Wall Street jargon. What investors then need instead is an ability to both disregard mob fears or enthusiasms and to focus on a few simple fundamentals."

I heard similar advice from Suze Orman when I first began investing: "Invest in Vanguard S&P 500 Index funds for the long term and you will win by minimizing transaction costs and management fees." Later, I read about Vanguard's approach from founder Jack Bogle's book *Common Sense on Mutual Funds*. His philosophy boils down to not trying to beat the market, but instead trying to match the market as closely as possible through broad index funds. The key is to minimize costs incurred by expensive active trading and adopting a buy-and-hold approach.

If you haven't already, being investing *today*! Invest in broad index funds. Pick those that have the lowest costs (expense ratios, taxes, trading costs) and hold for the long term.

5.14 Don't Attempt to *Look* Rich

In Thomas Stanley's book *The Millionaire Next Door*, he explains that those who look rich, drive expensive cars, live in large houses, and take exotic vacations may not actually be rich. They may *look* rich, projecting the lifestyle, but they may be spending all of their income and more besides. One of my doctor friends explained a similar situation with a fellow doctor in his practice.

"Dr. Smith regularly earns over $400,000 a year; however, he is now in his seventies and can't stop working because he had a divorce and owes money on a boat and his house. He doesn't have many assets to allow him to stop working." Stop and think about that. This doctor is in the upper 1 percent of all United States income earners, yet he is trapped. He is not free to choose to allocate his time as he may wish.

Let's compare this doctor with a janitor, Jeff, whom I heard interviewed on the podcast *Millionaires Unveiled*. Jeff never earned more than $40,000 a year — *90 percent less than Dr. Smith* — yet in thirty years of working he has accumulated a *net worth of $1.4 million and achieved financial independence!* He has the time freedom that the doctor can only wish he had. How is this possible? This janitor kept his expenses below what he earned and invested the difference.

Let's say that our janitor spent only $30,000 a year and saved $10,000 a year or 25 percent of his income. If he were to invest that at an 8 percent return, which is the return at which I've seen my own investments grow, at the end of thirty years he will have just under $1.2 million. If he keeps up that pace for another ten years his net worth will have ballooned to $2.8 million! Here is the amazing thing. He has gotten quite comfortable living on $30,000 a year. He is set for life!

5.15 Learn the 4 Percent Rule

The 4 Percent Rule states that if you conservatively invest your assets and withdraw only 4 percent each year, your assets will grow faster than you pull money out. For example, let's say after diligently saving and investing you have accumulated $1,500,000 in broad, low-cost index funds. According to the 4 Percent Rule, you can safely remove $60,000 a year ($1,500,000 x 0.04) to live off and still not draw down your principal.

If you can live off $60,000, your assets will be able to sustain your lifestyle indefinitely.

Your Financial Independence Number is the amount you must accumulate to generate the amount of annual funds to sustain your lifestyle. You no longer need to work and can enjoy time freedom. In this example, your Financial Independence Number is $1,500,000.

Once you have reached this, congratulations! You have achieved financial independence! What does this mean? Now you may choose to do the work if you enjoy it. You may also choose not to work. If you're passionate about creating movies, writing a novel, or traveling to another country to serve the locals — you can. You're not trapped into performing an activity just for the money it brings, but are free to do it solely for the joy it brings you.

5.16 Instructions — Calculate Your Financial Independence Number

To calculate your Financial Independence Number, we work backward from the 4 Percent Rule as follows:

1) Record your expenses using the budget categories mentioned earlier in this chapter.
2) Average Monthly Expenses: Add up your expenses for a period of three to twelve months, then divide by the number of months. These are your Average Monthly Expenses.
3) Annual Expenses: Multiple your Average Monthly Expenses by 12. These are your Annual Expenses.
4) Financial Independence Number: Multiply your Annual Expenses by 25. This is your Financial Independence Number.

Once again, I recommend checking out ChooseFI.com and its podcast to engage a financial community with great advice on achieving financial independence.

5.17 Increase Income by Increasing Value

The best way to increase income is to increase the value you're able to provide to the marketplace. You increase the value you provide to the marketplace primarily in two ways:

1) Increase sales
2) Reduce costs

I'll cover how to increase sales in a later chapter. For now, it's sufficient to know these are valuable skills for any organization. The way to increase your value is to work on two aspects:

1) Production (P)
2) Production Capacity (PC)

Production (P) is simply doing the work. If you get paid $10/hour for making a certain number of hamburgers, you can increase your Production (P) by working more hours to increase your pay.

Production Capacity (PC) is improving your skills and abilities to create more or better quality. If you watch a training video or observe a mentor making hamburgers, perhaps you can make 50 percent more hamburgers in the same amount of time, thus increasing your Production Capacity (PC), also known as your value. Eventually your income can be raised to match the value you create.

One of my favorite teachings by Jim Rohn is, "Work harder on yourself [PC] than you do on your job [P]," (emphasis added).

When I first read Bob Burg and John David Mann's *The Go-Giver* in 2004, I learned "The Five Laws of Stratospheric Success." The first and perhaps most valuable law in the book states, "Your true worth is determined by how much more you give in value than you take in payment."

This set me off in the direction of trying to create as much value as possible. This meant simultaneously increasing both my production and my production capacity.

★ ★ ★

Money is important because it provides food, shelter, clothing, and peace of mind, but you need to keep it in perspective. Make sure to keep your relationship to money healthy and clearheaded, especially as it relates to achieving your financial goals. The key is, no matter how much money you're making, to save or invest some part of it.

In the next chapter, we'll discuss a vital skill to improve your value to the marketplace – how to sell your ideas.

Take Action

- ☐ Outline your financial goals and take action immediately.
- ☐ Spend less by budgeting and tracking your expenditures.
- ☐ Start your retirement account if you haven't already. Commit to saving *a minimum* of 10 percent and seek to increase it when you can.
- ☐ Pay off your debt consistently and rethink your credit cards.
- ☐ Trim excess expenses from your lifestyle.
- ☐ Calculate your Financial Independence Number.
- ☐ Don't be afraid to enjoy, share, and be grateful when you spend money.

Read These Books:

- ☐ *The Richest Man in Babylon* by George S. Clason (My kids have read this already)
- ☐ *ChooseFI: Your Blueprint to Financial Independence* by Chris Mamula, Brad Barrett, and Jonathan Mendonsa
- ☐ *The Millionaire Next Door* by Thomas J. Stanley and William D. Danko
- ☐ *The Simple Path to Wealth* by J.L. Collins

6

SELL YOUR IDEAS

"The people who are crazy enough to think they can change the world are the ones who do."

Steve Jobs

Selling is important in all areas of life. This is not just for professional salespeople. You'll need to learn how to convey your ideas to succeed in conversations with others, team meetings, presentations, speeches, and, yes, client interactions. If you want to be able to reach your potential, you'll need to understand some level of sales and influence.

6.1 Influence Others

Influence starts with belief in your ideas. You can have brilliant ideas, but if you can't get people to take them seriously, your ideas won't get you anywhere.

At work, influence is often about personal relationships and trust. People don't care how much you know until they know how much you care. Once people understand you're concerned about their well-being, they'll open themselves to being influenced by you.

Matthew Kelly, author and founder of Dynamic Catholic, points out that "[t]he authentic self is genuinely interested in other people, while the ego is interested only in what other people can do for it."

You want to be appreciated, and so does everyone you meet. Being appreciated is one of the deepest human cravings. Sharing compliments is free to the giver, but, oh, how the receiver may covet and appreciate them! Mark Twain once said, "I can live on a good compliment two weeks with nothing else to eat." For one project we secured, I still recall how much it meant to me to receive genuine words of appreciation from a senior leader. When I'm in a leadership position, I try to do the same for the people I'm working with.

Is there someone in your life who may benefit from your appreciation? Take a few minutes — right now — to send them a brief message. Stop reading and do it now. You'll be glad you did, and they'll be happy to receive it.

6.2 Seek First to Understand

Seek first to understand, then to be understood. The way to do this is to listen until you can restate back to the person their views and why they are important to them. A good listener tries to understand thoroughly what the other person is saying. You may disagree with their point of view, but before you disagree, be sure to know exactly what you are disagreeing with.

President Abraham Lincoln shared his advice on influence: "When I'm getting ready to persuade a person, I spend one-third of the time thinking about myself, what I'm going to say, and two-thirds of the time thinking about him and what he is going to say."

Nature agrees: We have been given two ears but only one mouth.

6.3 Employ Effective Communication

You'll find yourself in a variety of professional environments interacting with people. The first step is to be aware of what you and the other person may be seeking to do. In general, all business conversation falls into four categories.

1) **Communicating:** This means both understanding and being understood by others. We all do it. How effective are you?
2) **Influencing:** Having an effect upon the opinions and behaviors of others. Do you actively seek to *influence* or are you passively *influenced* by others?
3) **Persuading:** Getting others to cooperate with you and getting them to do what you want them to do.
4) **Negotiating:** Getting the best deal you can for yourself, your company, or your family. Do you negotiate? How good are you at it? Think in terms of what the other person seeks to gain from the

situation. Focus on them first and show them how they'll get it from what you propose.

If you want to be a great communicator, plan and think through your communication in advance. The more important the conversation, the more you think. Tune in to WII-FM (what's in it for me) and talk in terms of how this will help them. Connect the dots. Ask questions to lead the conversation and control dialogue. Ask good questions and listen to the answers closely.

Communication is always important, but even when ideas or plans fail, maintaining good communication can minimize any negative impact to you and your reputation.

6.4 Ask for What You Want

If you've set your goals and desire something, what do you have to do to receive it? One of the most important actions is to ask for it. The Bible says, "Ask and it will be given to you; seek and you will find; knock and the door will be opened to you. For everyone who asks receives; he who seeks finds; and to him who knocks, the door will be opened." The key is to *ask*! This is good news! You can influence what happens to you and what you receive. You just need to set that in motion by asking.

When you ask, there are five important questions to keep in mind. *In italics I'll also illustrate how these apply specifically to sales.*

1) What do you want to happen? Are you looking to have someone go out on a date with you or do you want your boss to give you a raise? You've got to know your desired end result.

   Are you looking to make a sale? If your meeting goes perfectly, what do you want to happen at the end? You've got to be crystal clear on this before you go into a sales meeting.

2) Who is the right person to ask? It doesn't help for you to complain to a colleague about a work policy and ask them if they think it's fair. Ask

your boss or someone who can do something about it.

For complex sales, there are whole books written about how to identify and engage all the various decision makers and influencers involved. Suffice to say, you should ask someone who can say yes to your request. You'll tackle complex sales by gaining buy-in one decision maker or group at a time. Whom *you'll meet with will certainly impact* what *you'll be able to accomplish. You may have to go back and adjust your request to match what they can approve, and many times that's achieved simply by having another meeting with an expanded audience.*

3) Why do you want this? This only has to make sense to you and nobody else. Maybe asking this question will make you realize you don't even want it. For a relationship, it can't always be a one-way street — you taking and the other giving. If you're feeling selfish, examine if you have gone to the proverbial well too many times before asking for what you want. You may need to give more to the relationship and fill up the well before making withdrawal requests. Be aware of this balance.

In sales, I have earned most of my income by serving customer needs and generating sales for my company. I know this. My customers know this. I believe if there is nothing to lose by asking, and everything to gain, you should by all means ask. However, you'll increase your success if you focus on understanding their *why — what* they *desire will happen as a result of meeting with you. Remember, they're meeting with you because they have problems and needs and are hoping you may help them. Make* your *why to help them with* their *why.*

4) How do you ask for what you want? When I asked my son this question, he reminded me to ask politely. He's absolutely right! People listen to those they like and trust. Being polite is an easy way to be liked.

If you've also paused to think about how the other person or company will benefit from what you're asking them to do, connect the dots for them and show them how they'll benefit. Don't assume they'll make that connection. That responsibility is yours.

Once I realized that this is part of the value I bring to my clients, I got excited. I welcomed every chance I got to show them how I could help them get what they wanted with my company's resources. Generally, this boils down to them wanting more of something (revenue, income, productivity, etc.) or less of something (costs, time required, risk, etc.). This is how I continue to strive to be unique and add value to my clients and people around me.

5) When should you ask? Your timing may impact the outcome and response you get. For example, on a personal level, spouses, bosses, friends, family members, and customers are all going through different struggles that you'll never fully know about. Be sensitive that a "no" today may just be a "not at this time."

In sales, there are windows of time when people and organizations are ready to say yes. You can't control these windows, but you can do your part to learn about them and work accordingly. For example, for decisions over a certain dollar threshold that requires a board approval, when do they meet? When would they want to review all of your information and have all of their stakeholders' input and engagement completed by?

When I first started selling Cutco knives as a young college student, I had a hard time asking for the order. I had a hard time asking people to spend what I thought was a lot of money. When I remembered my purpose primarily was to gain experience and I was succeeding whether they said yes or no, I let go of the outcome — something I couldn't control — and instead focused on getting in front of more people. At the end of my presentation, I would ask if they wanted the knives. If they did, then I did all in my power to help them.

Later, in business, once I had a strong belief that my company provided literally billions of dollars of value to organizations every year, my focus shifted from a mentality where I felt I was selfishly asking them to do something *for me* to a mentality where I was trying to find out if and how I could *help them*. Nobody wants to be sold to. Everyone wants to be helped.

6.5 Leverage Meetings

I've attended and run thousands of meetings. Whether you're a participant or leading the meeting, here are a few tips to get the most out of them.

Maximize Meeting Value as a Participant

One of my HR directors, Jim, once provided valuable advice that I took to heart. He said, "When you are invited to a meeting or attend a conference, speak up! Ask a question or make a contribution. Don't passively sit in the background. Be known. This will mark you as someone of value." In addition to adhering to Jim's advice, I also realize that there is more value in speaking up early rather than later. The ones who bravely lead by offering their point of view early or asking a question tend to have an easier time doing so again later in the meeting. Seek to speak up within the first five minutes of a meeting or at the first appropriate opportunity.

When I was relatively new to my small start-up company, there was a division-wide meeting in which our CEO said a few words. Afterward, I knew he would take questions from the audience. I challenged myself to speak up. On my drive out to the event, I rehearsed my question to ensure it would demonstrate business acumen and also be a question whose answer I genuinely wished to know.

Sure enough, the time came, when after addressing the five hundred people in the room, he asked, "Okay, what questions are there for me from the group?"

My hand shot up. I was sitting in the front row, another practice I've learned, so his eyes lit up when he saw me. Pointing, he said, "Yes, you in the front row."

I asked my question. He paused to reflect and then answered it. Finished, he asked, "Who else?"

The crowd remained still. "Well, I guess that wraps it up then," he concluded.

A few minutes later, my vice president led the CEO over to introduce me to him! I have no doubt it was all because I chose to ask a question when others would not. By doing so, I raised my leadership ability in both their eyes and my own. Later, I was selected to enter into a training program where I was instructed by the same CEO. Years later, I was offered a massive promotion that I heard came with the endorsement of a few specific executives. It all started by speaking up!

Lead Effective Meetings

Undoubtedly, at some point in your career, you'll find yourself in a position where you will need to lead a meeting. Keep these tips in mind to make sure your meeting is as productive, efficient, and effective as possible.

1) Define the Start and End Time

Schedule it in advance so everyone knows what time it will begin and end. Then stick to it. This demonstrates respect for everyone's time. Typically, I use thirty- or sixty-minute increments. When possible, err on the side of longer than you need and work to finish early. When you accomplish your objective, end the meeting. People are always grateful to be given time back.

2) State an Objective

Peter Drucker says, "The effective man always states at the outset of a meeting the specific purpose and contribution it is to achieve. He always, at the end of his meetings, goes back to the opening statement and relates the final conclusion to the original intent." I include an objective on most meeting invitations I send out. This is an example of an objective I use for a first meeting with a prospective client: "The purpose of this introductory meeting is to share what our company has to offer, examples of where we've done it, and then learn about your situation to determine if we are a right fit for each other."

Here is an example of the objective of a reoccurring meeting to develop a project: "The objective of this biweekly touchpoint is to address development of <CUSTOMER PROJECT> to put <CUSTOMER> in position to be able to issue <WORK ORDER> by <DATE> to keep aligned with installation schedule." Note that the objective is always stated to be our mutual collective goal and not just what I may selfishly want.

3) Include an Agenda

I've found it helps to craft a simple agenda and issue it days in advance of the meeting, ideally as part of the meeting invitation. This helps all attendees know what to be prepared to discuss and what prep work they should do in advance. If there will be new people, I use introductions at the beginning to set the stage for the meeting. At the end, I make sure we determine the next actions. Everyone has put in their valuable time. Make sure something comes from that investment!

A five-point agenda can be particularly effective. Below is an example of one I've used for assessing the value of working with a potential vendor that would support my company.

AGENDA:

    I. Introductions
    II. MY COMPANY Overview of CUSTOMER Energy Savings
      & Project Overview & MY COMPANY plan for development
    III. VENDOR current support of CUSTOMER and locations
    IV. Scope of Work VENDOR has resources (systems, products,
      installation labor) and interests in providing for project
    V. Next Actions

4) Consider Your Seating

In kindergarten your teacher arranged where everyone would sit. It gave her more control and power to lead the room. Follow her example. When you sit with a client, some seats are better to lead a meeting from than others. Choose to sit at the head of a table or kitty-corner to your client's right or left and not opposite.

If your company has multiple people meeting with the client, don't have all of your company members sit on the same side of the table. This makes it seem like it's you versus them. Instead, divide up to integrate yourself with their team.

5) Begin with the End in Mind

What are you hoping happens as a result of the meeting? If you know your desired outcome, you can ask for it and you'll become infinitely more likely to receive it. Do this by thinking through what steps you may need to present in order to achieve the outcome you're looking for. Whether meeting with a client or a colleague, lay out your needs upfront.

6.6 Learn from Bill Clinton's Speaking Example

I was fortunate enough to attend the 2014 World Energy Engineering Congress in Washington, D.C. The keynote speaker was former president Bill Clinton. The U.S. Marine Corps Band played before the four speakers who preceded him, and it felt like a political rally. When he spoke, I couldn't help but be impressed. Regardless of political affiliations, Bill Clinton is a great speaker. I took the opportunity to both listen to his message and also to observe his manner for clues into his powerful personality. Below are three takeaways:

1) Begin in a Friendly Manner

Neutralize the audience. Even before Clinton took the platform, having the Marine Corps Band play before and between speakers harmonized the thinking and mental vibrations of the audience. This conditioned the crowd to be receptive. When first beginning to speak, he began in a friendly, self-effacing manner while telling a joke to poke fun at himself.

"Now that I'm not in politics, I can say whatever I want."
"Of course, now nobody cares."
"Unless, of course, your wife is still in politics."
"But then they only care if you say the wrong thing."

Each line generated laughter from the audience as he continued to win over the crowd.

2) Share Insights

To influence others, you must gain confidence and trust by sharing insights that may be valuable to them. Perhaps you're able to attend a conference and learn from it. Perhaps you meet someone famous. Share those experiences with others. When you do, you'll find you'll gain more credibility.

To illustrate, I'll share insight I learned from Clinton's speech. After the initial greeting, the moderator asked Clinton, "As president, you received lots of criticism. How did you handle it? Do you have a code or mantra we can learn from?"

In response, Clinton said, "I'd like to answer that with an example. There was a book I read many years ago. In it, the author says that when people are saying something to you it is about them, not you. For example, if I were to say, 'That tie you're wearing is the ugliest one I've ever seen.' You need to take it seriously, but not personally. What do I mean by that? If you take it personally, you'll tend to react emotionally maybe with anger or become defensive. Instead, take it seriously. It may be true or it may not be. Listen to it, hear if it can be helpful whether it is positive or negative. But remember also they said it because they needed to, and it was about them and not you. So maybe they are trying to be liked or put on an act to be tough. Take praise and criticism seriously, but not emotionally, and remember it is about them and not about you."

3) Tell Stories

People like stories. We all do. There is a reason Jesus taught using parables. The most effective leaders and influencers use stories and examples to illustrate their points.

Again, using Clinton to illustrate, after concluding his ugly tie example, he launched into a story:

"One of the people I've most respected and admired is Nelson

Mandela. Here is a man who, after he is out of prison and in political office, chose to put his captors in his cabinet and even had his jailer at his inauguration. Imagine that! Now Mandela and I were truly friends for twenty years. I remember once asking him, 'How did you get past hating those who had put you in prison?' Because he had publicly stated for the first eleven years of his imprisonment it was his hate that fueled him and kept him alive. So how did he grow beyond it where he was able to put members in his cabinet?

He said to me, 'For the first eleven years I was upset about all the things my captives had taken away from me — my freedom, my family, eventually losing my wife, and I came to the realization that they could take away all these things but there were two things they could not take away. Two things I would have to give them: my head and my heart. I chose not to let them have my head and heart but began to exercise them even in the confines of my prison.' ... When occasionally I would see Mandela after a particularly rough battle with Congress, he would say, 'Don't give them up,' and I always knew what he meant. That is what I learned from Nelson Mandela."

Learn to apply one of the most effective methods of connecting with others and influencing them, one that has been practiced for over two thousand years and is utilized by the most influential leaders of today: tell stories.

Beginning in a friendly way by using humor, staying away from politically charged topics, and sharing stories to win over the audience — these were qualities that made Bill Clinton an effective leader and great speaker. You can use them to become one too.

6.7 Public Speaking

> *"According to most studies, people's number one fear is public speaking. Number two is death. Death is number two. Does that seem right? That means to the average person, if you have to go to a funeral, you're better off in the casket than doing the eulogy."*
> — *Jerry Seinfeld*

How do you overcome the fear of public speaking? It's simple: speak. Follow the maxim "Do the thing you fear and the death of fear is certain." People fear that which they don't believe they're good at. Decide to become good at it. Join a local Toastmasters club. Seek out opportunities to speak in front of groups. Learn how to speak in front of others; take every chance you can. This decision will have an amazing impact on your life! Let's go over some great ways to approach public speaking.

Capture Audience with AIDA

Before you begin, your objective must be clear in your mind. Are you trying to inform, persuade, or entertain? There are many different styles depending on your objective. Below is an example of developing the body of a persuasive talk using the AIDA method.

- **Attention:** First, capture attention. Make a statement or ask a question to engage the audience.
- **Interest:** Explain facts, features, and details. Show how the idea will work.
- **Desire:** Show how they will benefit. "As a result of this, you will be able to do that."
- **Action:** Get the person to do something as a result of your activities or communication.

Five Rules for Effective Presentations

1) Introduce: Tell them what you're going to tell them. Explain: Tell them. Summarize: Then tell them what you told them.
2) Have a good opening and a good close, and keep them as close together as possible.
3) Practice!
4) Practice!
5) Practice!

Provide Your Introduction

If you're going to speak in front of a group, there may be a moderator or a master of ceremonies who will introduce you. Don't make the mistake of leaving it up to them as to how they'll choose to introduce you. This is a small but powerful opportunity to be positioned the right way. Provide the person introducing you with a written introduction that they can simply read word for word. Use it to establish your professional credibility prior to saying a word. This will warm your audience up and prepare them to have a positive view of you.

6.8 Instructions — Create Your Talk

Use the formula below for creating and delivering your next talk:

1) Determine the audience. Your audience will determine what you will be able to accomplish.
2) State your objective.
3) Brainstorm ideas of what you want to convey.
4) Organize these ideas to find the best three. Drop the rest. The more you say, the less they'll remember.
5) Develop supporting quotes, examples, and facts for these three ideas.
6) Use the "Windshield Wiper Method" to satisfy both the left and right brains of your audience members. Do this by alternating in providing supporting of your point with: fact, story, fact, example, etc.
7) Write out your conclusion — what you want them to take away.

8) Write your introduction; the introduction and conclusions should be mirrors reflecting the same goals.

9) Refine both intro and conclusion and learn them word for word. Learn your lines like a play. This captures attention and leaves a solid final impression.

10) Practice your speech and time the five portions — introduction, three ideas, conclusion — to ensure you have given appropriate time to each, while remaining within your allotted time.

11) Practice at least three times. I find it helpful to record myself on my cell phone using the Voice Memos app. Then I play it back. Once I learn my lines, I can focus on *how* I want to say them, placing emphasis on different words.

6.9 Select the Appropriate Sales Fit

"Nothing happens until somebody sells something."
— *Red Motley*

When I was growing up, my parents tended to avoid salespeople. I can understand why. People fear being talked into a decision or forced into an uncomfortable situation. What is the first image you think of when you hear the term "salesperson"? Many people conjure up images of a high-pressured, perhaps even sleazy, person who is out for their own self-interest.

Unfortunately, there is some truth to these clichés, and some have rightly earned this reputation. There are two types of sales: business-to-consumer (B2C) and business-to-business (B2B). The stereotypical bad salesperson behavior is most common in simple transactions, but it really comes down to the intent of the salesperson. Are they focused purely on their selfish interests of getting a sale or truly focused on helping the customer?

I'll provide an overview and illustration of each type of sale and mindset.

Business-to-Consumer Sales

Business-to-consumer (B2C) sales are typically simple, transactional sales. These are ones in which a seller and buyer may meet only once or at most a few times. These include salespeople in stores, door-to-door, and may include outbound call centers and telemarketers. A favorable quick decision is desired by the seller. These salespeople move quickly and believe if they ask a large number of people, enough will say yes for them to hit their goals. There is truth to this. People buy on emotion and justify with logic. Hence, the phrase, "It's a numbers game." When you want a larger TV, you'll convince yourself that it being on sale is a good reason to act now. As a salesperson, the biggest hurdle is inertia and people simply not taking action.

B2C Example – Cutco Knives

During my sophomore year of college, I met a guy, Neil, who would become one of my junior-year roommates. Neil was articulate and persuasive. When I asked him how he developed his skills, he told me, "I learned by selling Cutco knives. Why don't you try selling them over the summer?" I was studying to be an engineer and thought myself above such jobs.

That summer I was supposed to get an engineering internship. My dad had promised he had the connections to make it happen, and so I simply waited on him. Those connections fell through and I found myself working a manual construction job helping to tear down an old Phillips 76 oil refinery.

While there, I started reading biographies and autobiographies of Benjamin Franklin, Walt Disney, Thomas Edison, and others. I realized that at some point in their lives they all had been in sales. Next time I talked to Neil, I was ready to start as a Cutco salesman.

Turns out I fell in love with it. I had a blast meeting people and it was a lot of fun. Early on, I realized that Cutco would take anyone to sell on its behalf. Initial recruits were asked to make sales calls to family and friends as these were warm markets. Realizing this, I flipped the script and decided to help my family and friends get the best deal possible in terms of lower price or more free stuff. My belief had been that the knives were expensive. However, during one sales call, I arrived only to find out that one woman had owned her Cutco knives for forty years! Her knives were still in very good shape and better than most other knife brands I'd seen that were less than half as old. She wrote me a testimonial letter about how much she loved them. This letter, combined with my "Satisfied Customer" list, served as a powerful sales aid.

There's truth in the statement that sales are contingent upon the attitude of the salesperson, not the attitude of the prospect. Often if I had three sales calls lined up for a day, I felt very confident in my ability to have a "Grand Day," what Cutco called securing over $1,000 in sales for the day. To hit this would require averaging over $333 in sales at each of the three appointments. Not a bad average! This happened eight times over my two summers.

Unfortunately, I recall vividly the one time I did not place the customer's interest ahead of my own desire for a commission. I met with a little old lady in her townhouse. "Mark, these are very nice knives. I really don't do any cooking anymore so I don't need them, but if I buy them maybe my daughter will inherit them and use them." She was sweet and sentimental. For all my friends and family, I had helped them get the best value and as many free items as I could.

I could certainly use my knowledge to help her get the best value or provide a few free items, but it would reduce my commission. So I rationalized that she'd never know and I'd never see her again so there would be no harm. She never knew and wasn't disappointed, but I knew. For the price of dinner out for one, I sold my values that day. I never forgot and never did it again.

Business-to-Business Sales

Business-to-business (B2B) sales are typically larger purchases, over a longer period of time, requiring multiple interactions and often involving multiple people to reach a decision. The salesperson is dealing with a professional buyer. Short-term tactics don't work here. It requires initiative and engaging customers multiple times before concluding a sale. With the increase in size of the project comes added complexity as more and more people become involved.

For example, a marketing manager may have a budget and be able to authorize approval to spend a few thousand dollars in marketing without needing anyone else's approval. For projects exceeding a million dollars, you may need to deal with ten to thirty people, depending on the size of the organization, ranging from the person who signs the check to all the people who will be impacted, to a governing board for their approval.

I learned that if people like you, they'll listen to you, but if they trust you, they'll do business with you. You keep customers by delivering on your promises, fulfilling your commitments, and continually investing in the quality of your relationships.

B2B Example — The Chicago Cubs

You never know where you may find sales opportunities. It requires initiative and persistence, but when you do, you can reap uncommon rewards.

After graduating I decided to merge my mechanical engineering degree with my newfound interest in sales and pursuing a B2B sales career. I moved to Chicago to work for a company that provided and serviced heating, ventilation, and air-conditioning equipment, building automation systems, and security systems.

I lived three doors down from Wrigley Field on Sheffield Avenue. There was a 7-Eleven, an AmeriTech building, one other apartment complex, and then my building. It was an electric atmosphere. I often watched Cubs game on television in my apartment. I could hear the roar of the crowd cheering through my open window when the Cubs hit a home run.

Once I attended a game where it was "Ball Night." The first few thousand attendees received a free baseball. Midway through the game

DAD'S LITTLE BOOK OF WISDOM

there ended up being a close play at second base that went against the Cubs. One of the fans threw a ball in protest. Soon, all of the balls started raining down onto the field as they tried throwing them at the umpire at second base who had made the call. The game had to be stopped as they cleared the field of all the baseballs. That night ESPN ran story after story about how Wrigley couldn't control its fans.

It so happened that the person in charge of security for our office had attended the same game. The next day we were both talking about the game. I said, "I wonder if Wrigley would be in the market for a new security system?" Sure enough, it took a long time to get a hold of its director of security but eventually we were able to see him. During the next off-season, we installed nineteen CCTV cameras and a DVR for recording activities at Wrigley.

As Opening Day approached, I asked our new client if there was any way we could get tickets to the game. He said, "You don't need tickets. Just tell them you're here to see me." On Opening Day, I nervously showed up with our head of security, my boss, and my boss's boss. I walked up to the attendant taking tickets and announced, "We're here to see M____." He called in on the radio and after the affirmative response, waved us in. We walked up and checked out the newly installed security system for ten minutes, then went and found available seats to watch the game.

Whether you're self-employed, a professional salesperson, or just willing to take a risk, if you put in the effort through initiative and perseverance, you can certainly enjoy both financial abundance and once-in-a-lifetime experiences.

6.10 Use Sales Tools to Succeed

When you're in sales, you're essentially in business for yourself, with your employer as your top client. The most valuable asset you have is your time. It's important to have a way of prioritizing your time among all competing interests. Below are some sales tools that have been vitally helpful during my professional sales career.

Top 10 List of Opportunities

Here is how it works.

- List ten or more opportunities where you can put your time and effort.
- In another column, list your benefit or payoff. In sales, this would be the amount of the sale.
- Write down the expected finish or close date.
- Write down your next action and when you will perform this action.
- Sort your list based on the largest payoff, closest to closing.
- Begin performing the action for your number one ranked project. Then, when that's done, move on to number two and so forth.

By looking at this list and updating it regularly, you'll see progress. More importantly, you'll have peace of mind knowing that regardless of the outcome you achieve, you're doing the best you or anyone else could reasonably expect for the time invested.

Magic Words to Schedule Meetings

Large, complex sales require consensus among many people. The goal from meeting to meeting is to gain momentum. In any group, there are key influencers. Their voice and opinions will sway others.

Gaining momentum first requires demonstrating how you can help someone see the value you can bring. In arranging initial meetings and subsequent ones, I've found the following few magic words work wonders: "What is your availability?"

These magic words have been the source of many, many of my appointments with clients and internal team members. Once they reply with their availability, I'll review my calendar for an open slot and specific time within their range that works for me.

Let's look at an example conversation.

"John, I'd like to talk with you about what it is we do, how we've helped others like you, and then learn a bit about your situation to see if we might be a fit for each other. What is your availability on the 14th or the 16th to have an initial conversation?"

"Mark, I'm open the morning of the 16th from 9:00 a.m. until noon."

"Great, let's do it at 10:30 a.m. I'll send you an invite to lock it in on both our calendars."

Through this approach, you will be able to fit more in and will be more productive.

Book Your Calendar

Since your time is the most valuable resource you have, the way you allocate and schedule it will go a long way toward ensuring your success. In dealing with others, I've found whoever has the busier schedule tends to have the meeting scheduled around their availability.

Your level of sales success will be in direct relationship to your ability to manage your time and by extension your calendar. This is vitally important when you're prospecting through many initial conversations seeking to uncover a good fit between another company and yours or when leading multiple internal teams to develop simultaneous projects.

Airlines double-book seats knowing that they'll have cancellations. Do the same. If you have an appointment and another comes along, don't say no too quickly to a meeting request. Frequently, someone will have a conflict pop up, causing one of the meetings to fall away. If you're left with both, you may need to be the one to request rescheduling the less important, i.e. non-customer, meeting.

6.11 Overcome Obstacles

In sales, you'll deal with a lot of rejection. As in any endeavor, you will have many obstacles on your way to achieving the outcomes you desire. What is the secret to overcoming them? Don't avoid them. Face them and resolve them as quickly and thoroughly as possible.

Get the Training You Need

I've found that my lack of confidence evaporates when I know what to expect and what is expected of me in a situation. If you get the training you need, you'll feel more confident and perform better. Don't rely on your employer or anyone else. Take full responsibility to ask for the help you need and seek and pay for it as necessary. You'll be glad you did. Your paycheck will reflect your skill and effort.

When I was at the start-up company, I began receiving sales coaching from a guy named Tim I had gotten to know through my local Toastmasters club. The biggest area Tim assisted me with was helping me realize that not only did I have weaknesses, I had blind spots that were holding me back!

One of my blind spots involved taking initiative. I was defensive at first. I said, "Tim, I do take initiative. Every time my boss tells me what to do, I do it."

He replied, "Mark, that's why it's a blind spot. You don't realize that that isn't taking initiative. You are waiting for direction."

It's laughable to me now, but I genuinely just didn't realize I was subconsciously shifting ownership of my success from my shoulders to my boss's.

Tim supplied affirmations and exercises to strengthen my mental resolve in these areas. This was really the first time I religiously used affirmations. Why? Tim was my accountability coach and he was going to ask me about them! Much later I would use affirmations for other goals. I wish I had started using these so much earlier!

Understanding my blind spots and changing my mental focus was a turning point in my career and life. If you haven't already, I urge you to get coaching or an accountability partner. This all starts with a personality assessment. You can complete one through Gallup's CliftonStrengths, an online assessment at www.gallup.com. This can save you years of frustration and enable you to earn more and achieve more much faster than it would otherwise take you.

Reward Yourself

I have used many mind tricks to distract myself from how unpleasant a task is. For example, if I have set a goal of making five prospecting cold calls, as a reward for making these dials, I'll allow myself to read fifteen minutes of a book. It doesn't matter what the reward is as long as it's something you enjoy. Focus on your desired reward. This will pull your mind away from overthinking the unpleasant task. Almost like a tractor beam, your reward will pull you through the feared task to the other side where you can celebrate by enjoying your reward.

Steel Yourself Against Opposition

Not everyone will understand you. In fact, many will not. The bolder or more daring your undertaking, the more you may have to brace yourself against the naysayers.

Be careful not to expect much support for your ideas, especially from those whom the status quo serves to benefit. Nonconformity will always generate external pressure to conform. If you perform beyond the norms, the systems will adjust and try to make you normal. An example of this is a salesperson crushing their yearly sales number. The following year, they may find themselves with either an outrageously high sales target or a reduced territory with additional salespeople in the mix to help harvest this fertile market.

Seek Not Validation from Others

One of the traps I often found myself falling into was seeking the approval of others. Perhaps it's natural. As William James said, "The deepest principle in human nature is the craving to be appreciated." The danger in this approach is offered by Dodinsky: "If you persistently seek validation from others, you will inadvertently invalidate your own self-worth."

★ ★ ★

Selling yourself requires overcoming unsureness and understanding what you are actually offering someone. Managing their expectations and creating trust are key to being a valuable asset. Now that you've learned how to influence others, in Chapter 7 we'll explore how to make decisions yourself.

Take Action
- ☐ Go out and share an idea with someone to help lock it in.
- ☐ Join a local Toastmasters club. Seek out opportunities to speak publicly.
- ☐ List your ten biggest opportunities right now.
- ☐ Create an agenda for your next meeting.
- ☐ Conduct a personality assessment to determine your strengths.
- ☐ Get the training you need to succeed.
- ☐ Identify something you want for which you will need to negotiate.

Read These Books:
- ☐ *The Go-Giver* by Bob Burg and John David Mann
- ☐ *StrengthsFinder 2.0* by Tom Rath
- ☐ *The Speed of Trust* by Stephen M.R. Covey

7

THINK THROUGH YOUR DECISIONS

"Your life today is a result of your thinking yesterday. Your life tomorrow will be determined by what you think today."

John Maxwell

The highest-paid and most valuable work in America is thinking. Why? Because of all the things that people do, thinking has the greatest possible consequences. The better you think, the better decisions you make. The better decisions you make, the better actions you'll take. The better actions you take, the better results you'll get. The better your results, the better the quality of your life and work. Everything begins with thinking.

As author Denis Waitley posited, "The winners in life think constantly in terms of 'I can, I will and I am.' Losers, on the other hand concentrate their working thoughts on what they *should* have or *would* have done, or what they *can't* do."

How do you move away from a life drifting from one experience to another and, instead, take control of your life? You do so by thinking and deciding upon what you want your life to look like and where you're going. You may be stuck in your head — we'll talk about how to get unstuck and how to trust yourself to overcome doubts that may be holding you back. There are times when you aren't ready to make a decision and even times where you may not be the one to make the decision and need to ask for help. I'll share with you how to handle each of these situations.

7.1 Know Where You Are Going

Charles Kettering, once head of research at General Motors, liked to say, "A problem well stated is half solved." If you at least know the problem you intend to solve, you're halfway to solving it. In other words, knowing which direction to go is half the work, and you can do that work sitting in a chair and thinking. I'm reminded of that famous scene from *Alice in Wonderland* after she has gone down the rabbit hole:

> Alice: "Would you tell me, please, which way I ought to go from here?"
> Cheshire Cat: "That depends a good deal on where you want to get to."
> Alice: "I don't much care where."
> Cheshire Cat: "Then it doesn't matter which way you go."

Steps to Take When Stumped

When you don't know what you want and when you're feeling stumped about what direction to move in, you'll likely feel lost. What's the solution? Recall from chapters 1 and 2 that the key to finding success is constantly remembering your desires and goals. Remember that if you set a strong enough goal, it will pull you of its own accord. Your desire will power you to out-think any resistance or obstacles. To determine what to do next, start with your top goal and think about what steps you can take to move it forward. Act upon it. When you've exhausted this, move on to your next goal. Keep doing this to identify a goal you can take action on and move it forward.

Practice Patience

Perhaps you have to wait on someone else. Ask yourself, "Have I done all I can do to move my goal forward at this time?" If the answer is yes, move on to your next goal and wait a bit for things to progress naturally. Very few important goals rely solely on one person.

I've found holding a regular session at the same time every week with an important project's stakeholders helps ensure I'm not missing anything. If the next step is out of your hands, let yourself relax for a period of time.

Prioritize Values

Are you happy with what you have or where you're going? If the answer is yes, great! If the answer is no, consider what you might choose to do differently. Remember, the more you do of what you've done, the more you'll have of what you've got. As the adage goes, insanity is doing the same thing over and over again, but expecting a different result.

Our core values help to guide our behaviors. It's not hard to make decisions when you know what your values are.

One of my prized values is freedom. Yet, I also value giving and contributing to others. I feel a sense of obligation to share my abundance. "Of those to whom much is given, much is required," echoes through my mind. I have created a high level of sales, which has enabled me to earn a level of time freedom. One of the ways I'm using this time freedom is to write this book. I chose to do this in the first place because I value wisdom passed through books and writings. The ideas I have read have helped me immensely. It's my fervent desire that they likewise aid you.

7.2 Instructions — Think on Paper

Thinking on paper helps with clarity. You'll recall in Chapter 2 you were instructed to pull out your own ideas and thoughts by writing. Journaling helps you literally face yourself by externalizing your thoughts and goals. The best part is, once you write out your feelings, goals, and decisions, you've actually taken some meaningful action toward realizing your goals. Writing down a simple plan in a journal can be the first step of your thousand-mile journey.

There are several established processes for helping to come up with better ideas and methods of making decisions. Below are examples and instructions on how to think on paper in order to make better decisions.

Goal Setting

Recall from Chapter 2 the importance of writing down your goals. Record what you want and your plans to accomplish them. These plans are best kept in a place that can be referred to often. I've found the use of a journal is an excellent tool for this. In my journals, I have a page for goal ideas. Then on a separate page I write out the single goal at the top of the page with greater definition or plans underneath it.

Brainstorming

Nobel Prize–winning scientist Linus Pauling stated, "The best way to have a good idea is to have lots of ideas." This is why, at the beginning of an undertaking, it's worthwhile to put all ideas on the table, practical and impractical, for scrutiny and consideration. Brainstorming with two or more people is a popular approach, but it can also be applied as an individual. Remember that while we may start with many ideas, the goal is not to have many ideas, but to have one idea that works.

The 6 Whys

One method is to "Ask the 6 Whys." Ask yourself, "Why do I desire this?" Write down your answer and then ask again. And then ask again until you're six levels deep. You'll find your true motivation may be below the surface. By uncovering it, you will understand the real reason you may want something or feel conflicted about it.

For example, I did this exercise again today, trying to understand why I was having a difficult time writing on a certain subject. After several rounds I came to the realization that these sections involved writing about my opinions and deeply personal illustrative examples. I realized these are much harder for me to write about because I fear they may be criticized. Once I understood that it was my unconscious seeking to protect me from being vulnerable, I was able to weigh the pros and cons of including what I was writing. Then I could consciously decide what I felt comfortable sharing.

Four Decision-Making Questions

After you decide what to do, you may have difficulty taking action. This is common. There may be the fear of the unknown holding you back. Below are a series of four questions to help you weigh the risk and rewards.

1) What's the worst thing that could happen?

2) What's the best thing that could happen?

3) What's the most likely thing to happen?

4) Knowing what I know, am I willing to take the risk?

Decision Tracker

One tool that I've used is a "Decision Tracker" to write down what I want and what action I'm taking. I leave space to come back later and record the results. Was it a good decision? Or should I have chosen differently? The results often surprise me. It turns out that things rarely turn out as poorly as I might have feared. Over time, this practice has both improved my decision-making and increased my confidence in making decisions.

As discussed in Chapter 3, this is an excellent way to overcome FEAR. No need to write down what you *don't* want to happen. Keep your mind focused on what you *do* want to happen. I've found that over 90 percent of the time I either made the right decision, was glad I acted, or both!

7.3 Be Congruent

There is no surer way to lose self-confidence and the trust of others than to profess one thing and do another. The following story I originally heard from a priest during his homily.

A mother and daughter visited Gandhi. The mother said, "Gandhi, my daughter is addicted to sweets. Would you speak with her about how the addiction is not good for her? I truly believe hearing it come from you will have a big impact."

Gandhi said, "Tell me more. Please describe her addiction to sweets and how bad it is."

The mother told him.

Gandhi listened patiently and then said, "Come back in three weeks."

Puzzled and a little disappointed, the mother took her daughter and left.

Three weeks later she returned. When she again was able to speak with Gandhi, she asked, "Will you speak with my daughter regarding her addiction to sweets? I am sure that speaking with you will mean a great deal."

Gandhi took her daughter and went off for a long while. When they returned, the daughter went up to the mother and said, "Momma, I will change. I will no longer eat so many sweets."

The mother was thrilled. This was the result she was looking for. She said, "Gandhi, thank you so much for talking with my daughter about her addiction to sweets and persuading her to stop. But why couldn't you have done this three weeks ago when we first came?"

Gandhi replied, "Because three weeks ago, I too was addicted to sweets."

Be congruent. Don't ask people to do something you haven't done or wouldn't do yourself.

During those times when I've slipped and was not being congruent, I felt uncomfortable. When I sensed another person picked up on it, I would feel embarrassed and ashamed. I've found the best thing to do when I slip is to apologize to the person impacted and seek forgiveness as quickly as possible.

Believe me, it's better not to carry around the burden of trying to keep up a façade.

If you happen to notice another person saying one thing and doing another, it's very tempting to judge them. Though you may not fully trust them while they continue that behavior, I'd encourage you to not think too harshly of them. They are most likely feeling insecure themselves.

7.4 Trust Your Gut

Decision-making doesn't have to be complex. In his book *Blink*, Malcolm Gladwell shares the insight that a snap decision takes into account all of your unconscious perceptions and, many times, is superior to a longer analytical decision. Trust your gut, it's a type of thinking!

This is often most important if you want to do something unconventional. Thinking might lead you to not take the risk but listening to your gut will tell you to ignore conventional wisdom. I first heard this next quote by George Bernard Shaw from my friend Randy, who certainly lived the maxim himself as he started up two companies, "The reasonable man adapts himself to the world: the unreasonable one persists in trying to adapt the world to himself. Therefore, all progress depends on the unreasonable man." So, at times, be unreasonable!

One of my favorite poems is *The Road Not Taken* by Robert Frost in which he highlights how our decisions lead us into totally new lives, especially when we take the unconventional route — the road less traveled:

> *I shall be telling this with a sigh*
> *Somewhere ages and ages hence:*
> *Two roads diverged in a wood, and I —*
> *I took the one less traveled by,*
> *And that has made all the difference.*

7.5 Overcome Doubt with Decision

Another way of looking at your decisions is that each one moves you closer to your end goal. Tony Robbins reminds himself constantly that "every action I produce successfully yields a result I may learn from." One of the biggest things to overcome is inertia. Fear keeps us stuck and prevents action. Ideas often seem harder in our heads. We spend precious energy and time contemplating a task, rather than just doing it in less time and with less energy. Whether that's taking a trip, writing a blog post, or presenting in front of a group, afterward these things almost always seem easier. This is when thinking can slow you down.

General Norman Schwarzkopf, leader of the U.S. forces during the Gulf War, knew about making decisions. When commanding troops during a war, each wrong decision he made carried with it the possibility of using millions of taxpayer-funded aircraft and tanks and, more importantly, endangering the lives of servicemen and -women. What advice does he employ for handling this pressure? "When in doubt, make a decision anyway. Making no decision can be catastrophic, while even a bad decision creates movement, action, and can be corrected upon." In summary, the best thing to do is the right thing. The second-best thing is the wrong thing. The worst thing is nothing.

Iterate Toward Your Goal

A simple board game is finite in its outcomes. It has rules and an explanation of how to determine a winner. The game of life doesn't have such a definition. Life is an infinite game with endless possibilities. If you want to win an infinite game, the only way is to continue to play. Make a ton of moves. The opponent in the game of life is time. The way to win is with speed. The person who iterates the fastest, wins.

Every great leap forward in your life comes *after* you have made a decision of some kind.

One of the most monumental decisions in my life happened when I finally decided I was done working in my then position. In response to my tirade about how unhappy I was at work, my wife responded, "Mark, I don't care if you work at the local grocery store. I just don't want you to be miserable all the time."

With her blessing, I made a clear decision. In my journal I wrote, "I will be employed in a different position within ninety days." The next time recruiters called, I listened. One of them led me to my next job and continued my career progression. This only happened *after* I made this decision to act.

7.6 Know When Not to Decide

There are times to act and times to deliberate. Be aware that you don't always have to make a decision right away. In those cases, it's important to instead put your time and effort into determining when exactly a decision actually needs to be made. Until that time arrives, gather relevant information. This prepares you to make the best choice by the deadline of your decision. What holds people back isn't always a lack of information. As an anonymous humorist once said, "It ain't what you don't know that gets you into trouble. It's what you know for sure that just ain't so."

From years of selling and seeing how people make decisions, the following adage proves true: "People tend to buy on emotion and justify with logic." This also holds true with how we make decisions. When money is involved, be careful that you're not swept away in an emotional moment that you'll later regret. If you do, you may find yourself overrun with credit card debt or paying much more for a car like I originally did. Before making an important decision, it's crucial to back up and first decide if your state of mind and the circumstances are right to even be making a big decision. If it's not the right time, hold off.

7.7 Ask for Help

If you're thinking about your next steps or your plan of action, don't be afraid to ask for help. It's important to seek out those in the best position to make the decision or advise you. For example, if your question has to do with money matters, ask someone who is in a better financial situation than you. Thinking is important, but if you do it all alone, you might be missing out on some very important insights.

Ask the Right People
In his book *Principles,* Ray Dalio lays out how he assembled a team that enabled him to build the largest hedge fund in the world, Bridgewater Associates. He advises to increase credibility for certain decisions by involving those who have a proven track record in those areas. The goal isn't that you have to have all the knowledge yourself, but to surround yourself with people in the best position to make the decision. Bridgewater goes as far as having baseball cards for each associate that shows their track record of projects and decisions. Not everyone's vote counts equally. They exercise weighted decision-making. The votes of those who have performed better in that area count for more.

Ask Intelligently
I've found the best leaders are experts at asking questions. Focus more on asking intelligent questions than on answering questions intelligently.

If you're faced with a tough decision and are looking for guidance, ask God for help. James 1:5 advises, "If you need wisdom, ask our generous God, and He will give it to you. He will not rebuke you for asking." This is a subtle reminder that we all need guidance.

★ ★ ★

You've now learned how to think through your decisions. The use of thinking on paper will help you make decisions and learn from them. You've learned when to decide and when not to, how to do it on your own, and how to ask others for help.

Who are some of the people you'll reach out to? Who wants you to succeed and who do you want to see succeed? Your family and friends, of course. In the next chapter we'll explore your most important relationships.

Take Action

- ☐ Start a Decision Tracker in your journal.
- ☐ Schedule regular time each day or week to plan or review your active decisions.
- ☐ Next time you face a tough decision, write down the 6 whys and try to get to the heart of the decision and your needs.
- ☐ Listen to your gut when making a decision.

Read These Books:

- ☐ *As a Man Thinketh* by James Allen
- ☐ *Thinking for a Change* by John C. Maxwell
- ☐ *Principles* by Ray Dalio

8

CONNECT WITH YOUR FAMILY AND FRIENDS

"People will forget what you said, people will forget what you did, but people will never forget how you made them feel."

Maya Angelou

At this point you should feel confident in your ability to accomplish your individual and professional goals. You've learned the attitudes and skills to be successful in the workplace and the mindset needed to succeed. However, if you don't have solid relationships with those closest to you, many of your accomplishments may feel hollow. Let's look at the vital steps in fostering relationships with your family and friends.

8.1 Cultivate Relationships

Building relationships requires a few key ingredients:

- Time investment
- Listening and understanding
- Taking an interest in others
- Building others up
- Loyalty and integrity

Invest Time

Whether friend or family, love requires a willingness to invest time and attention into another person. The greatest gift you can give to a person is the purity of your attention. As you think through your most important relationships, ask yourself, "How much am I sharing myself?"

At one point, my work was consuming more of my time and attention than I would have liked. My wife commented, "Mark, when you aren't traveling and are physically present, I still feel like you are not mentally present. I feel alone." In examining my values, I realized I needed to make a change. I did. Much of the reason was to give time to my wife and kids.

Listen and Try to Understand

Before sharing, listen. Author and businessman Stephen Covey captured it simply, "Seek first to understand then to be understood." This is an area I have struggled with. Often, I'll feel an urge to speak about my own message first. What I've learned is interactions will go much smoother when the person you're interacting with feels heard and understood first. If you aren't already, try listening more.

Take an Interest in Others

Do you want to have more friends? Dale Carnegie's book *How to Win Friends and Influence People* captured many important principles. One is that you can make more friends in a month by being interested in them than in ten years by trying to get them interested in you.

I read Carnegie's book for the first time the summer before my freshman year of college. Eager to apply his lessons, when I met people during freshman orientation mixers, I would discreetly write down their names and a few details about them. Later, I would make the effort to visit them in their dorms. Being able to recall their name, remember a bit about them, and demonstrate a willingness to learn more led me to quickly developing a diverse group of friends.

Build Others Up

What you talk about matters. Are you discussing the faults and offenses of other people? If so, this relationship is not building you into the best version of yourself. It also may not last. How can it? In the back of both of your minds is the concern that someday the other may be discussing your faults. This type of relationship lacks trust. Instead, if you're helping each other grow, even if it's by candidly addressing your faults or theirs and areas of need, the relationship can be life changing. Several times I've sought out people whom I respected for advice and feedback on my performance. Many of my deepest friendships and relationships have grown from a desire to improve myself and in turn offer any assistance I can to the other person. One of those friends who has had the most impact on me is Brian.

I first met Brian in August 2013. At the time we were working for separate companies. After meeting others in his organization, I made the decision to have my company place our resources behind his to be selected for a multimillion-dollar state project. I had heard about Brian from others in his company — they spoke almost reverently about him. When he walked into the room and began speaking, all eyes were riveted upon him. He didn't disappoint. As if we were watching Michael Jordan step onto the court, we could all feel the room's energy level go up, and we knew we were going to win.

On that first day, Brian spoke with focused intensity and asked insightful questions to pull out of the team key success factors before guiding us to formulate a winning strategy. His confidence drawn from past successes and experiences inspired all those in the room.

After a long day of working on our plan, the group went to dinner. During dinner I shared with Brian that he reminded me of the book I was re-reading, *The Go-Giver*. He said it sounded like his philosophy. "Mark, I'm continuing trying to live my life to bring value to others. I also want my last day to be my best. That means I'm continually looking to be better — better at sales, better in my faith, better as a husband and father." He had been his company's top salesperson and had an incredible track record of sales accomplishment. He was an irresistible personality. I wanted to learn more from him and mold my personality from what I could learn from him. When I returned home, I mailed him a copy of *The Go-Giver* and actively sought to cultivate a friendship with him.

Brian saw more in me than I did in myself. At this point in my career, the largest sale I had been involved with was $250,000. Brian observed my speaking abilities, which I actively had been developing through Toastmasters over two years and made a decision that changed the trajectory of my life. He asked me to make the crucial closing arguments to the selection committee as to why they should select our team for the $44 million project — the team for which I was only a subcontractor!

It was the most important two-minute speech of my life. For hours I honed and practiced it.

We won. The selection committee told us our presentation was like watching a movie.

That project is a crowning highlight in the careers of many individuals involved. For me, the biggest things I took away was an increase in self-confidence and a friendship with Brian.

Brian and I began to hold weekly one-hour sessions in which after reading a chapter of a book we'd discuss what we learned, how it related to our own previous life experiences, and how we might apply the lessons in our lives. Session after session, book after book, year after year, our friendship grew and we both continued to improve personally and professionally.

I didn't realize all the self-limiting beliefs I had been harboring. Through our conversations Brian continually challenged my thinking and beliefs about myself and what was possible. He also affirmed to me, "Mark, you are having just as big of an impact on my life." His confidence allowed me to continue to grow and my career skyrocketed with his mentorship.

It's my hope that you can find a friendship like this one. Remember, it doesn't just happen. Meaningful relationships require initiative, intentionality, and time.

Be Loyal to Those Not Present

The Bible states, "Do not judge that thou shalt not be judged." I remind myself of this often when tempted to think ill of another person. Benjamin Franklin voiced similar views, "I will speak ill of no man ... and all the good I know of everybody." How can you put this into practice? One way is to demonstrate loyalty by defending those who are not present. Said another way, the best thing to do behind a friend's back is to pat it. The habit of speaking up about the virtues of those who are not present and defending them from attacks is sure to eventually come around. This provides two benefits. First, it solidifies respect for you from the person you defend. Second, it garners the respect of the person to whom you're speaking. You're demonstrating your character in that moment. Seek out opportunities to sing another's praises. Silent gratitude isn't much good for anyone.

8.2 Help Others Get What They Want

"Life's most urgent question is:
What are you doing for others?"
— Martin Luther King Jr.

One of my favorite Zig Ziglar teachings is: "You can have everything you want in life if you'll just help enough other people get what they want." When you shift your thoughts away from what you want to reflect on what others want, you'll find yourself with a new ally. In business, I've attended hundreds of conferences generating thousands of first impressions. Most people are tuned into their favorite radio station — WII-FM (what's in it for me). If there isn't immediate value in the interaction for them, they quickly move on. This is shortsighted. Instead, aim to provide value to those in your network. A smaller network of personal walking ambassadors can work miracles in your favor. You create this small army by caring more about them than you do yourself.

To be happy, help make others happy. Take the time to make a difference in a person's life. Ask, "What can I do to help another?" When starting out, don't worry about quantity. Help one person at a time beginning with the person nearest you. Ralph Waldo Emerson observed, "It is one of the most beautiful compensations of this life that no man can sincerely try to help another without helping himself ... serve and thou shall be served."

Have you ever been in a rut? One of the best ways to forget your own problems is to help someone else solve theirs. This giving approach paradoxically helps you expand. Love only grows by sharing.

One of my favorite activities is to gift a book that I feel will benefit someone. Even more meaningful have been the times when I've read the book at the same time as another person and then talked about it with them regularly. For example, I've lost track of how many times I've given away *The Go-Giver* and offered to set up one-on-one mini-book club discussions. Several times during a two-week span, we'd talk about the fourteen chapters. I've given it out to friends, family, clients, co-workers, and even my company's CEO. I do this because I genuinely want to help them, yet I continue to experience deep and profound benefits from unexpected sources every time I do.

8.3 Select Close Friends Wisely

Life can be difficult. Don't go at it alone. Have at least a handful of close friends and maintain those friendships by investing time. You don't need lots of friends, just one or two really close ones. The ones you're closest to may rotate in and out over time as you go through different stages of life. That's normal. But they'll always be part of you and your friendship will likewise impact them. Climbing the mountain of life will be best remembered for and by the people who made the journey with you.

As you move through the stages of life, choose your friends wisely; you will become like them. Warren Buffett warned that, "You will move in the direction of the people you associate with." That's why it's important to choose friends whom you admire and whom you hope to be more like one day. As long as you're hanging around amateurs, you will think like an amateur. Successful people fill their lives with positive thoughts about themselves and others.

When choosing whom to be around, don't join an easy crowd. You won't grow. Go where the expectations and the demands to perform and achieve are high. This will help you to become a better version of yourself. Keep away from people who try to belittle your ambitions. Small people always do that, but the really great make you feel that you too can be great. Since whatever you focus on grows, think often of your friends and seldom of your enemies.

8.4 Choose to Grow for Others

You're either growing or dying. Motivational speaker Charlie "Tremendous" Jones said, "Five years from today, you will be the same person you are today, except for the books you read and the people you meet." I've found this to be absolutely true. Grow by reading and attending seminars. Invite people out to lunch. New information leads to growth. As I write this, I'm at a conference in Pittsburgh, where I just heard a four-time Super Bowl–winning player speak. At the same conference I met a number of people who may positively help with creating business and additional relationships. Open yourself up to as many growth opportunities as possible.

Activate the Law of Cause and Effect

Oftentimes the world will treat you as a mirror to yourself. This can be both good and bad. When I'm generous and giving, I feel good and attract others. Unfortunately, when I believe that I have nothing to give or gain, I've found I shut myself off. Both become self-fulfilling prophecies. People will treat you how you expect they will. If you change your self-image, it will change how you act and how people treat you. This is the Law of Cause and Effect.

Remember, the goal is not to be superior to other people, but superior to your previous self. This illustrates the concept of CANI: Continuous and Never-Ending Improvement. It also sets you up for a lifetime of work, for you can always get better. When we measure ourselves against another person, we may feel we are falling short or perhaps we are smug in our self-satisfaction. Neither of these serves us in the long run.

Invest in Yourself for Your Loved Ones

You can't change people. The only person you can change is yourself. But by changing your behavior, you can often change how people treat you. Gandhi said, "As a man changes his own nature, so does the attitude of the world change towards him." So model the change you desire to see.

When you invest in becoming the best version of yourself, you're also giving those around you whom you love the greatest gift you can give. The more knowledge and skills you acquire and develop in specific areas, the more you can bring to your loved ones in your capacity as a father, mother, husband, wife, brother, sister, cousin, parishioner, neighbor, friend, etc.

8.5 Learn from My Story — Speaking as Best Man

I recall a time when my focused growth in my speaking abilities allowed me to give my brother a unique wedding gift and at the same time teach my son.

When my brother asked me to be the best man at his wedding, I was honored. But I was also scared. I knew I had to give a speech. I could choose to do the minimum — stand up and mumble a few awkward words and sit down as quickly as possible — or I could choose to deliver a meaningful speech to honor my brother and his new bride. I was grateful my two years attending Toastmasters meetings and learning public speaking had prepared me to choose the latter.

After writing out the speech, I needed to practice it the night before. I asked my then ten-year-old son to help me. I did this because I wanted him to see the work and effort I had to go through before being on stage in front of everyone. My son would go to various areas of my practice room and listen to me give parts of the speech. Then he would tell me if I was loud enough.

Throughout the speech the roar of laughter from the crowd told me they heartily approved. I turned to read my brother's reaction. His face was slightly flushed but with a broad smile. This told me I had achieved my desired delicate balance of sharing personal insights that let him and the rest of his close family members know that he is loved and understood. I was glad I had put myself in a position to give this unique gift to my brother. It was also special for me to have my son there to see the preparation.

When you choose to invest in developing your knowledge and skills and practice the disciplines outlined in this book, you never know who may seek your help in the future. When those dearest to you are able to benefit thanks to you, you'll be glad you made that investment!

8.6 Be the Right Spouse

Marriage is like a pair of shoes. As you get accustomed to each other, you become a better fit for each other. It takes work by both parties. You can't easily change your spouse, but you can change yourself and how you treat your spouse. A lot of pressure can build up in finding the right person to marry. Going into marriage, it's important to remember there is no such thing as the perfect partner.

Study Your Spouse

If you married your spouse when you had the equivalent of a high school degree of knowledge about them, keep studying them until you get your doctorate. During your relationship, there will be times when you disagree with each other. That's normal and natural. However, unless the circumstances are dire, don't disclose private details about your relationship to family and friends. Keep those details private.

The most valuable word in marriage is commitment. Be committed to stick through thick and thin. If you need help and have to talk with someone, seek out a professional. This will help the recovery much better than having well-meaning family and friends simply take your side.

Raise Your Kids

Harmon Killebrew, a Hall of Fame baseball player, said, "My father used to play with my brother and me in the yard. Mother would come out and say, 'You're tearing up the grass.' Dad would reply, 'We're not raising grass. We're raising boys.' "

It's important to keep the main thing the main thing. That means investing time doing things with your kids and taking an interest in them. Choose to make them a priority with your time.

For a long period of time I scheduled at least one shared activity with each of my kids every week. Oftentimes this has been reading with them. As the kids became older, we'd discuss views on what we had just read. At other times it has been video games, the Magic the Gathering card game, board games, card games, and volunteering.

8.7 Bring Out the Best in Others

I often use the phrase "iron sharpens iron" with my close friends to remind both myself and them how grateful I am for how they help me to become the best version of myself. They quickly reply, "Mark, it goes both ways." Below is one such example.

I met Steve in 2012, when we were both selected to be part of our company's executive leadership program from two different divisions. Each year the company would choose twenty-four people to attend from over ten thousand employees. We were randomly placed in a small group and immediately hit it off. Steve joined the company when his original employer was acquired. As the company was divvying up responsibilities, instead of opting for a comfortable assignment, Steve voluntarily decided to be an area director for Florida to gain experience managing union employees. That decision struck me as the type a strong leader would make. He immediately garnered my respect and admiration.

After a few years out of contact, I was developing a project for a ski resort that resulted in engaging his division. Our paths crossed again on a conference call with several people on the phone to discuss the business opportunity. As soon as it was over, I dialed his number to reconnect with him on a personal level.

Steve shared with me his personal development plan and desire to become an operational vice president. It required honing sales skills. I had not been a manager and sought his expertise on leadership. We agreed to read a book on leadership together and discuss. Once a month, we would talk for an hour about the book and real-world leadership lessons. After three or four months of doing this, he asked, "Mark, would you want to come to the wild side and join my division?"

I knew when he said wild side, he meant stepping into a leadership role. This was a big career jump for me. I went from being a solo contributor to being responsible for leading eighty people including sales, sales managers, and a call center. I also had responsibility for profitable, durable growth of 12 areas and 136 district offices, stretched across 17 states. Again, Steve saw more in me than I did in myself. With his encouragement along with that of my other mentors, I accepted the offer.

Shortly after I joined Steve's division, our mutual boss was promoted, creating an opportunity for Steve to also be promoted. I called our COO and advocated on Steve's behalf. Unfortunately for Steve, he wasn't selected; nor was he the next time. I kept encouraging him. Three years later, he left the company to finally take on a coveted VP position at a comparable company. All of his years of preparation had paid off. I felt so proud and happy for him.

Seek out others to befriend whom you respect and admire. Help them any way you can. Help propel them to even higher heights. Help bring out the best in them. Advocate for them. Become a personal walking ambassador for them. By adopting this giving mindset, you'll be amazed at what life gives back.

8.8 Learn from the Story of Edison, Ford, and Firestone

Thomas Edison, Henry Ford, and Harvey Firestone had a friendship that benefited each of them throughout their lives. The extensive story is told in James Newton's book, *Uncommon Friends*, which I highly recommend. Below are three impactful pieces that I took away from it.

1) Support Dreams

Thomas Edison supported Henry Ford before anyone else did. This meant a lot. Newton asked Ford if he recalled their first meeting at a convention of the Association of Edison Illuminating Companies in Manhattan Beach in Brooklyn, New York, in the 1890s.

Ford replied, "I should say I remember that day. It was a turning point for me. Mr. Edison listened to me very patiently. Then he banged a fist on the table and said, 'Young man, that's the thing. Your car is self-contained, no boiler, no heavy battery, no smoke or steam. Keep at it!' You can imagine how excited I was, the man who knew most about electricity in the world — my boyhood idol — telling me my gas car was better than an electric car! He was the first to give me real encouragement that my dream would work! Well, that boyhood idol became my manhood friend."

2) Add Value by Educating Your Customers

Before they were friends or even business associates, they were salesman and customer. Harvey Firestone recalled his first meeting with Henry Ford:

Firestone said that one day a young Ford came into his buggy shop with a plan for building a low-priced car that farmers and workers could afford. Ford said he was building it in a shed behind his house and he needed four tires. He was looking for solid-rubber tires — the old carriage tires that were in use then — but Firestone recommended trying a new type, pneumatic tires, with air in them. His company had just ordered a few. He took Ford back to the warehouse stockroom to see if he could find them. He did, and Ford bought them. As he left, Ford said, "I may be back for more."

Years later, Ford put in an order for eight thousand.

3) Value Key Friendships

As a token of his friendship with Edison, Ford gave him the first car off each new assembly line. And when Edison's Menlo Park laboratory burned down in 1914, Ford showed up with a check for $750,000 to help him rebuild.

In 1915, Edison, Ford, and Firestone journeyed to the West Coast with their wives to visit the San Francisco World's Fair. They had such a good time that the families set off on the first of their annual camping trips.

I can't help but wonder what effect the association of each of these great men had upon the others. I often tell my kids, "You pick your friends and then you'll become like your friends." Similarly, as it states in Proverbs 13:20, "Walk with wise men and you will become wise, but the companion of fools will fare badly."

Who are you surrounding yourself with?

8.9 My Dad

When I was a teenager, I was pretty hardheaded. I would get into arguments with my dad about how he wasn't giving me enough respect and latitude to make my own choices. Little did I realize at the time, I was behaving exactly the opposite of how I would if I were actually a responsible person!

We'd be at a deadlock with neither looking to admit their fault. Yet without fail, my dad would choose to soften his stance first. He would humbly come apologize to me for his portion of our disagreement — even when I may have been 80 percent at fault. He'd cry and tell me how much he loved me. I'd soften too. We'd hug. He was the dad. He chose to be the bigger person. That isn't just what it means to be a dad, but that is what it means to love someone. To be willing to "see past the speck in your neighbor's eye to see the log in your own." Then to humbly act upon it to ask for forgiveness.

I've tried to follow his example. Not perfectly, but still I try.

My dad gave me much affirmation. He always told me, "Mark, I love you and I'm proud of you." He said it enough times that as a kid I just accepted it and knew I was secure in his love, and didn't need to do anything to earn that love and appreciation.

I didn't realize how lucky I was until I read the book *I'm Proud of You* in which Tim Madigan describes the interaction between him and Mr. Rogers — yes, *the* Mr. Rogers. Madigan explains how he so desperately wanted someone to be proud of him he asked a virtual stranger to just say that he was proud of him. That made me realize that I was lucky to have my dad. I also acknowledge that despite my dad's support, many times during my career I too desperately craved appreciation from others.

Sales can be a very rewarding profession — it can also be merciless. My sales production was easily measured by a number. Early in my career, when my sales were down, I felt like my worth as a human being was also down.

This is a trap!

Perhaps you need someone to tell you that they are proud of you. If so, let me reach out through these pages and tell you, I'm proud of you! I'm proud of you for reading this far! I'm proud of you for the work and growth you've already done on yourself! And I'm proud of you for the positive impact you're having on those around you!

Now it's your turn. Both gratitude and appreciation are only of value when shared. Find someone and express your genuine gratitude. Your few words may be the very thing that another person needs to hear at that moment.

★ ★ ★

Choose with care the people you are closest to because, over time, you'll become more like them. Make sure to invest the time necessary for those relationships to thrive. Not only will you derive great joy from them, but these relationships and people will serve to assist you in all other areas of your life.

In the next chapter we'll discuss an even more vital relationship — the one you have with God.

Take Action

- ☐ *Be* the friend you wish you had: Call someone. Invite them to lunch, dinner, or an evening out.
- ☐ Commit each month to inviting three to five people to join you for lunch, dinner, or an activity.
- ☐ At the end of an enjoyable time together, schedule another one for some time in the future.
- ☐ Identify and keep close those people who inspire growth and confidence, personally *and* professionally.

Read These Books:

- ☐ *How to Win Friends and Influence People* by Dale Carnegie
- ☐ *The 5 Love Languages* by Gary Chapman
- ☐ *The 7 Habits of Highly Effective Families* by Stephen R. Covey

9

FOSTER YOUR FAITH

"The moment we open ourselves up to God's plans is the moment miracles begin to happen in our lives."

Matthew Kelly, *Dynamic Catholic's Best Lent Ever 2017*

I'm glad you're reading this. This is the chapter I believe that makes all the other ones truly worthwhile. Why? Your relationship with God is more important than your relationship with family and friends. It's more important than all the accomplishments and accolades you may receive. It's more important than all the toys you accumulate or vacations you go on throughout your life. How you foster your faith will impact every facet of your life. But how can you grow in faith? Just like with any relationship: time.

Despite being raised by two loving parents and having them demonstrate their commitment to their faith, for years I was more of a "check-the-box Catholic." I would dutifully show up each Sunday to check the box that I attended. I would check the box for politely doing what I was asked, such as giving a percentage of my income to the church and to charities benefiting those in need. But I didn't let it go much deeper.

I was doing the minimum and I wasn't investing time getting to know Jesus on a personal level. As a Christian, I started to feel like an impostor because I still didn't feel comfortable talking *about* Jesus or *to* Jesus. Why? I don't know really. Perhaps it's because the world has become one in which we live at the surface and don't really go deep. Turn on any television, watch movies, check your newsfeed or social media, and you'll be bombarded with images that serve to lure you into the lifestyle they are selling.

For me, I felt a powerful draw toward what success looks like — a prestigious leadership company position, a nice car, a large house, and exotic vacations — all to announce to the world that I was successful!

Once I got all those, then I would be successful. *Then* I would be good enough. *Then* I would be worthy. *Then* the world would celebrate me.

That is the trap. The world wants you to always want *more*. It wants you to feel that you aren't enough as you are. A desire to earn more and achieve more can be a noble pursuit, but what it comes down to is your fundamental *why*. Is it to impress the world? If so, you'll never receive the satisfaction that each of us so deeply craves.

But God loves us where we are and as we are. Jesus is the example sent to show us how to live and love. I'll share more of my faith journey through this chapter. For me this is both deeply personal and uncomfortable — but sharing this is why I feel I was called to write this book in the first place.

9.1 Listen

The first part of faith is being open to hearing God's call. Listen for your instructions. It's hard to listen when we are overwhelmed with the busyness of life. This is, in a way, what is meant by "the devil's in the details." When we become lost in the details, we lose sight of the big picture of what God is calling us to do. It's only when we shut out the world that we reenter that classroom of silence to hear His will.

Inside this state of faith, we are empowered to take risks that lead to creative and meaningful breakthroughs. Canadian novelist Arthur Stringer observed, "Genius seems to be the faculty of having faith in everything, and especially oneself." To do this requires opening your heart and listening.

I recall when I purposely began to open up my heart to listen to the Lord and how it continues to transform my life. For several Lents, my wife signed up for Dynamic Catholic's Best Lent Ever email series. Every day for forty days she would receive an email from them with a three to five-minute reflection video. She would occasionally forward on ones that had significance to her along with a sentence or two about how it impacted her.

I found myself enjoying these thoughtful notes from my wife. I began reading the video transcripts so I could quickly gather the gist of what was being said, in order to write back to her. A funny thing happened. The messages started to get through to me. I felt my spirit awaken and began to pray more intently than before while asking God for His guidance.

At the end of Lent 2018, I didn't want to stop. Matthew Kelly had spoken about the use of a Mass Journal. I had heard of the concept before but couldn't seem to establish its use as a new habit. Now I was committed. I ordered a Mass Journal to have a special place to record weekly lessons from Mass. I've faithfully used it every week since to help me ask and listen to God's guidance.

Are you ready to listen God's calling for how you may do His will? Who might you send a note to about your faith that may awaken their faith? How about giving them a book? Who knows, maybe you will have a profound impact on a loved one's life!

At the end of this chapter, I'll share how Jesus built upon my willingness to hear Him to transform my business life.

9.2 Act as a Conduit

According to Webster's dictionary, "A conduit is a channel for conveying water or fluid." I recall at a Toastmasters meeting when one of the speakers suggested we should act as conduits not of water but of the spirit of God to do His will. Shift from a self-focus to a God focus by realizing that great works are done through us not by us. A relevant prayer I often recite is, "Thou are the Potter, I am the Clay. Mold me and make me after thy will." Similarly, I repeat, "God is with me, God is helping me, God is guiding me." Really listen to that inner voice for guidance. Act upon it. Trust you are in God's hands. God places beautiful desires deep within us. Have faith knowing God wants to give you the power to attain the desires that are placed within you; you only need to allow Him.

9.3 The Attitude of Gratitude

Adopt an attitude of gratitude because whatever you focus on grows. Focus on that for which you are grateful. Do this and your blessings will multiply like the loaves of bread Jesus shared when he fed the five thousand. As Uncle Ben told Peter Parker before he became Spider-Man, "With great power comes great responsibility." Use your God-given power and gifts wisely.

9.4 Connect to the Universe's Energy

All the universe is made up of energy. Everything you see — including yourself — is made up of energy. Solid matter is nothing more than energy moving at a certain speed. We are all vibrating at speeds so fast as to be undetectable to the human eye. The universe is made up of energy. But where does this energy come from? I believe the answer is God.

Use Your Sending and Receiving Station

God and Holy Spirit can permeate everything. Where do ideas come from? They are simply synapses firing in our brain. In his book *Think and Grow Rich*, Napoleon Hill discusses the concept that each person's brain is both a sending and receiving station. You may think of communication as the words and gestures you say and make when you're with another person. This is true. However, what you don't say communicates as much as or more than what you say. You're giving off vibrations and energy levels that are subconsciously being picked up by those around you.

Feel Those Vibrations

After meeting someone, you have probably found yourself thinking, *I have a good feeling about that person*, or conversely, *I don't have a good feeling about that person.* You're receiving the vibrations subconsciously about that individual. Keep this in mind and take them seriously. Your thoughts matter. Dogs read people and can tell if they're afraid. If you're afraid, vibrations are sent out. Think about what you want, visualize what it is you desire, and you're much more likely to realize it as the people and things around you receive those positive vibrations. If you live in fear, so will those around you.

Act in God's Image

You are created in God's image and likeness. This means you are endowed as a creator. You are unique — an artist. When you fully embrace who you are, and your own talents and abilities, you can create amazing things.

No matter how big or small any organization is, it began with a single person and a single idea. Where did that idea come from? God. If that idea is placed in fertile soil, it grows and bears fruit. Aim to be fertile soil. Be selective so as to not dissipate all of your energy on multiple endeavors, but rather choose a few and nurture them into existence. Examples may include: running a marathon, starting a book club, forming a movement within your church, developing a major business deal, or planning financial security for your family.

9.5 Act in Faith

What does the Bible say about faith?

- "I can do all things through Christ which strengthen me." — Philippians 4:13
- "According to your faith be it unto you." — Matthew 9:29
- "If ye have faith ... nothing shall be impossible." — Matthew 17:20
- "Have faith in God for verily I say unto you, that whoever shall say unto this mountain be thou removed and be thou cast into the sea and shall not doubt in his heart but shall believe that those things which he saith shall come to pass, he shall have whatsoever he saith." — Mark 11:22–23
- "If thou canst believe, all things are possible to him that believeth." — Mark 9:23
- "For as he thinketh in his heart, so is he." — Proverbs 23:7

Your belief about the outcome at the beginning of an undertaking is the single most important factor in determining the likelihood of achieving it.

Take a Leap of Faith

In the movie *Indiana Jones and the Last Crusade*, Indiana Jones comes to a dark chasm as he seeks the Holy Grail. His treasure map depicts people walking on air to cross it. He swallows hard, closes his eyes, and takes a big step forward into a wide abyss. His foot is greeted with an invisible bridge. He is then able to cross, but only *after* he was willing to literally take a leap of faith. This leads us back to that first step of the thousand-mile journey: to take the first step, even on solid ground, you must have faith in yourself that you can and will complete your journey.

Let Your Faith Guide You

Through your belief and faith in a higher power, you tap into a source of energy that will fuel you to accomplish great works. John D. Rockefeller, founder of Standard Oil — the first real corporation — was a fervent Baptist and believed he was doing God's will by organizing labor to bring low-cost kerosene to the masses. Later he felt his wealth was entrusted to him to do God's will, and so he focused the second half of his life on charitable giving.

Eliminate Inferiority

The greatest secret for eliminating inferiority complexes is to fill your mind with overflowing faith through prayer. One way is to repeat the Romans 8:31 verse, "If God is for us, who can be against us?" Listen to your inner voice, then go forth with confidence. Believe in yourself!

What holds us back? Robert F. Kennedy answered this question, "The danger of futility; the belief there is nothing one man or one woman can do against the enormous array of the world's ills. ... Yet many of the world's great movements, of thought and action, have flowed from the work of a single man."

Don't Wait to be Perfect

Perfection is a trap. In the Bible we learn that Moses committed murder and King David had a soldier killed and committed adultery. Yet God chose them to do His will. Jesus chose Peter, who was flawed, to be the leader of the Catholic Church. Heed God's call and don't worry that you're imperfect. He's used to working with imperfect people, and if you wait around until you're perfect, you'll never get started.

9.6 Let Your Light Shine

What holds you back? There are days you may be grumpy and feeling out of sorts. You may have woken up on the wrong side of the bed and feel things aren't going your way. You find yourself in a rut from which it is difficult to get out. This poor attitude can lead to poor actions and eventually a weakness in your character if it goes unchecked. As Marianne Williamson writes:

> Our deepest fear is not that we are inadequate. Our deepest fear is that we are powerful beyond measure. It is our light, not our darkness, that most frightens us. We ask ourselves, who am I to be brilliant, gorgeous, talented, fabulous? Actually, who are you not to be? You are a child of God. Your playing small doesn't serve the world. There's nothing enlightening about shrinking so that other people won't feel insecure around you. We are all meant to shine as children do. We were born to make manifest the glory of God that is within us. It's not just in some of us; it's in everyone. And as we let our own light shine, we unconsciously give other people permission to do the same. As we are liberated from our own fear, our presence automatically liberates others.

Since you've stayed with me this long, I'll let you in on a little secret. While I've felt called to write a book for as long as I can remember, my fears held a choke hold on that desire. My limiting self-talk would say to me, "Mark, who do you think you are to write a book? You haven't done anything. No one would want to hear what you have to say." So, I went to work on becoming what I believed other people wanted me to be — to look successful. After over two decades the message changed but the intent remained the same: "Mark, who do you think you are to write a book and brag about your accomplishments?"

The writing above helped me overcome those self-limiting beliefs. So did my increasing faith. So did my then twelve-year old daughter, who wrote and published her first book, *Diary of a Cell*, when she was in seventh grade. She let her light shine and inspired me — her dad — to do the same.

I have worked very hard to replace my unhealthy self-limiting beliefs with messages of faith. My wish in sharing this book with you is that it helps you even in a small way to do the same. Will some people not understand? Yes. But do you want to live less of a life to avoid the opinionated view of others? Presumably not.

I often remind myself that we are called not to judge. If others want to judge me, that is between them and God. As for me, I pray very hard to remove judgment when it crops up in my thoughts or especially in my words. A wonderful thing happens when you remove judgment — you can be genuinely happy for a friend or family member's success! It's truly an amazing feeling to be genuinely happy for the successes of another. Surround yourself with these people and you can do incredible things simply by removing the negativity that may otherwise hold you back.

Your God is not looking for you to be a small version of yourself. He wants you to be the best version of yourself. Jesus said of himself, "I am the light of the world." I love that. Remember, we are created in God's image. If Jesus is the light of the world and we are called to be like him, aren't we called to do the same and share our own light? Can you imagine Jesus shrinking so that the Pharisees didn't feel bad? Can you picture him saying to himself, "I could calm these rough waters, but if I do my friends (aka disciples) will think I'm a show-off." Of course not! He also didn't flaunt his power as evidenced by how He chose to give up His life for us.

9.7 Do Small Things with Great Love

Do you want to adopt a successful mindset? Focus on giving and creating. You may feel your contribution is not important, but that's not for you to judge. As the saying goes, "Not all of us can do great things. But we can do small things with great love." So, undertake those small things that are before you with great love.

The world may never know your greatest contributions. Perhaps it's calling friends and colleagues to let them know how much you appreciate them, perhaps it's cooking a meal so your spouse doesn't have to, perhaps it's using your positive energy and creativity to entertain your family after being stuck at home for weeks. For these acts you won't receive a promotion — and you may not receive a thanks — but if you are doing it out of love, the act is a reward in itself. Smile to yourself knowing you are on the path to a good life.

Theologian Albert Schweitzer observed, "The only ones among us who will ever be truly happy are those of us who have sought and found a way to serve."

I'll close with an illustrative favorite poem.

"What! Giving again?" I asked in dismay.
"And must I keep giving and giving away?"
"Oh no," said the angel looking me through,
"Just keep giving till the Master stops giving to you!"

9.8 Attain Peace of Mind

In Proverbs 16:3, we're instructed, "He who plans a thing will be successful. Happy is he who trusts in the Lord." Don't drift. *Make plans!* But also remember that planning is good and necessary up to a point, but you will find God in the now. God lives in the eternal now. Take action, and recognize you can't control the outcome, but if you trust in God every outcome is the right one. This will help you to have peace of mind.

Focus on controlling what you can control and letting go of the rest.

One of the best reminders of this is the Serenity Prayer,
The Serenity Prayer is a powerful tool for restoring peace of mind.

God grant me the serenity to accept the things I cannot change,
the courage to change the things I can,
and the wisdom to know the difference.

Be Comfortable in Your Own Skin

Many times I've said to friends that what I want for my kids is for them to be comfortable in their own skin. Of course, this is easier said than done. We are surrounded by the opinions and unstated standards of what is acceptable and what is not. Orlando Aloysius Battista set a high bar to aspire to and I believe there is truth in his words: "You have achieved the pinnacle of success as soon as you become uninterested in money, compliments, or publicity." This means that success, to some degree, is doing something because you think it's the right thing to do, and being guided by a strong internal compass. Unconditional self-acceptance is the core of a peaceful mind.

Follow Your Internal Compass

Without this strong internal compass, it's easy to be caught up in pursuing what the world says is success. But the success Jesus teaches is not of this world. In Mark 8:36, Jesus challenges us by asking, "For what shall it profit a man, if he shall gain the whole world, and lose his own soul?"

To build up your peace of mind, direct your focus.

In Philippians 4:8 we're instructed, "Whatever is true, whatever is honorable, whatever is just, whatever is pure, whatever is pleasing, whatever is commendable, if there is any excellence and if there is anything worthy of praise, think about these things."

Fill Your Mind with Thoughts of God

When your mind is full of God, there is no room for worry. Fill your mind with thoughts of God rather than with thoughts of fear, and you will get back thoughts of faith and courage. Dynamic Catholic founder

Matthew Kelly describes it as all humans having "a God-sized hole." He says that you can't fill the hole with a career, a person, or money. Only God will be able to fill the hole.

9.9 Instructions — Use a Mass or Worship Journal

I admit I don't know enough about my own faith, let alone all the other religions in the world. However, I truly believe if most people lived what they profess to believe, the world would be a better place. Don't just check the box with your faith like I did for decades. This lukewarm faith didn't serve me, and it won't serve you either.

How are you developing your faith now? Is it working for you? If not, perhaps it's time to experiment with something new. I urge you to invest time in your faith. Maybe it starts with something simple like showing up to a service and taking notes.

Following Lent in 2018, I decided to adopt the practice of using a Mass Journal advocated by Matthew Kelly. The concept is simple. Attend your weekly service and pray the following prayer, "God, show me one way that I can become a better version of myself this week!" Then each week during your worship service, listen for the one thing. It may be during the first reading, the second reading, the gospel, or the sermon. Or it may be nothing that's said, but because of the thoughts on your mind that you walked in thinking and praying about, an idea and course of action may pop into your head. Write it down and commit to doing that one thing.

For me, doing this was often uncomfortable. One such action I committed to was to approach the pastor of my church with an idea to form a Lenten Book Club. This stretched me beyond my comfort zone. To approach him meant I might be rejected. I avoided it for a week, but the same idea popped into my head the next week as well. This time, my inner voice said, "Mark, I'm not giving you another idea until you complete the one I already gave you." This was enough to spur me to action.

Other times, an idea you may write down will be to develop better daily habits. Perhaps the one thing will be an area of focus for the week, such as being more intentional about doing a Holy Moment each day. A Holy Moment is where you listen to what God is calling you to do in the moment and do it. Can you imagine a world where all Christians and others of faith went to their weekly services with pen and journal in hand asking for what they were being called to do that week, and then did it?! That would be a world I would love for my kids and future generations to inherit.

Like any other habit, maintaining a Mass Journal takes practice. As you'd do with a muscle, you strengthen the habit through exercise. While praying, pray to be made stronger. While we will never reach perfection, it's in the striving that we become better versions of ourselves.

9.10 Learn from My Sales Partner, Jesus

Seven months after stepping back into a direct sales position, I was struggling. I was feeling pressure to get a big win and all of my opportunities seemed to be shriveling up. I had a small opportunity that became less attractive the more I looked at it, but it was the best shot I had. I clutched it closely and hoped I could follow through.

Around the same time, I read Nick Foles's book, *Believe It.* In it, the 2018 Super Bowl MVP tells his football story, which was impacted by his faith journey. Foles was traded from the Philadelphia Eagles to the St. Louis Rams. He wasn't a good fit for the offensive scheme for his new team. He dropped in the depth chart and football was no longer fun for him. He was ready to quit playing football and walk away from a $10 million contract.

His family and friends convinced him that he was quitting for the wrong reasons and to give it another shot. Foles agreed, praying, "God, everything I do, let it be to glorify you." He was reunited with his old coach Andy Reid in Kansas City, ego in check, and accepted a role as a backup quarterback for the Chiefs.

After the season, the Eagles brought Foles back as a backup quarterback to Carson Wentz.

Late in the season, Wentz went down with an injury and Foles had to come in off the bench. Many wrote the Eagles off heading into the playoffs. Despite being a number one seed, they would be underdogs throughout their magical playoff run. Against all odds, at the Super Bowl, they won over the heavily favored New England Patriots and Tom Brady.

At the post-game interview, Foles said, "I wouldn't be out here without Jesus in my life. I tell you that first and foremost. I don't have strength to come out here and play this game like that and that's an everyday walk. I mean we have struggles as people and you know that's just been my rock and my family."

As I finished reading Foles's book, I said to myself, "Why not me? I'm not a professional football player, but why not me? I can be an instrument of God's will like Foles. If I have any success, let it be Your will and not mine." I had always prayed to God, but despite being raised Catholic, I did not feel comfortable praying to Jesus.

I had this realization while sitting in my car and turned to the empty passenger seat and prayed, "Jesus, I would like to take you as my sales partner. Please guide me. Any success I receive, let it be to bring glory to you."

Then I listened in the silence. I believe God speaks to you and me. The question is, "Are we listening?" This time I was.

I felt a little voice inside my head saying to let go of the opportunity I was so desperately clutching. I could feel Jesus directing to me to let go and have faith.

Soon after, driving to a lunch with my boss on the way to meet with the regional general manager, whose approval I needed in order to submit an important proposal, he told me:

"Mark, we need a win."

"Yeah, I just have a feeling this is not a good fit for us."

"What do you mean?"

"If we submit, we'll likely be short-listed, which means we will spend more time preparing for an oral interview. That will tie us up. Even if we win, this is now such a small project our company won't really consider this a win. As much as I really want to get a first project and be on the sales board, I feel we should pass."

"Okay, if that's how you feel."

At the lunch with our regional general manager, right after signing our submission authorization, I told him, "Thanks for your approval. This is really hard to say, but I think we'd be better off not submitting this. As much as I personally want to add value by winning a project, I feel it is best for our organization's resources that we pass." We discussed for a bit and he concurred.

This was a difficult decision, but I was guided by my sales partner, Jesus. I took a leap of faith. I released my grasp on the illusion of security and declined to submit the proposal.

As you know, sometimes when God closes a door, He opens a window. It doesn't even have to take very long. At the conclusion of that lunch, my manager told me that since I now had some bandwidth, I should call someone who might represent a good business opportunity.

That opportunity turned into a project worth over $100 million.

★ ★ ★

By listening to your faith and actively applying God's will, you'll find your life transforming. He is preparing you to be an instrument of His will. Be humble enough to listen. Be courageous enough to act on what you are called to do.

In the final chapter, we'll discuss how His will enables you to lead others through your example.

Take Action

- ☐ Schedule ten to fifteen minutes each day to spend time with Jesus; pray, read, or write during this time to increase your faith.
- ☐ Take a Mass or Worship Journal to your weekly religious service and say the following prayer, "God, show me one way that I can become a better version of myself this week!" Then listen for the one thing and write it down. Act upon it.
- ☐ Do small things with great love. Consider volunteering at a local food bank or nursing home.

Read These Books:

- ☐ *The Biggest Lie in the History of Christianity* by Matthew Kelly
- ☐ *Believe It: My Journey of Success, Failure, and Overcoming the Odds* by Nick Foles
- ☐ *Resisting Happiness* by Matthew Kelly

10

LEAD BY YOUR EXAMPLE

"Be more concerned with your character than your reputation, because your character is what you are, while your reputation is merely what others think you are."

John Wooden

Growing up, hopefully you had one or two good role models. Regardless of what you may or may not have had in the past, it's up to you to chart your future. Your willingness to accept full responsibility for who you are and where you go will be the mark of self-leadership. There are tools that will guide you. It will require utilizing many of the attitudes described above alongside your growing skills and abilities. As you grow, people will look to emulate you. Let your actions speak louder than your words. This may attract opportunities to lead — perhaps informally, as a go-to person on your work team or on a project, or formally as a manager or director at your company with direct reports. As you continue to develop, keep increasing your skills.

10.1 Lead Yourself First

Charles Lindbergh was arguably the most famous person alive during the early twentieth century, thanks to his completion of the first solo transatlantic voyage in his plane, *the Spirit of St. Louis.* While he was world-renowned, it was not fame he craved. It was his independent mindset and fixed convictions that motivated him: "I'll take adventure before security, freedom before popularity, conviction before influence."

Leadership starts with a vision of yourself, and a vision of the future. You'll attract others into your life through the person you become and the vision you share. You can't base your life and actions on other people's expectations. Lead yourself first. Develop good habits and stick to them, because integrity is the ability to make and keep promises to ourselves. A true sign of who you are is how you behave when nobody else is watching.

What is the antidote? A mindset that's not blaming external circumstances and coming up with excuses, but rather continually asking, "What can I do?" Focus on controlling what you can control. Take those actions and you'll be amazed as the world makes a path for you. It all starts with self-leadership.

10.2 Keep a Journal

For over twenty years I have maintained the practice of writing in my journal and have amassed a collection of them. Other than family photos, I consider these journals my most prized possessions.

Below are the subjects I've found helpful to include in my journals over the years:

- Goal Ideas
- Goal Plans
- Books to Read
- Books Read
- Movies to Watch
- Movies Watched
- Gift Ideas
- Family Notes
- Interviews
- Book Notes
- Balance Sheets
- Decision Trackers
- Holy Moments
- Customer Meetings
- Emotions
- Illustrations
- Reference Documents
- Training Notes
- Conference Notes
- Notes to Make Better Journals

Real leaders are ordinary people with extraordinary determination. When you have an experience, good or bad, are you capturing the lessons of what you did well or would do differently so as to improve in the future? In my journal, I've made it a point to ask three questions regularly following experiences like a sales call, interview, or important meeting:

1) What did I do well?
2) What did I learn?
3) What would I do differently?

You don't want to have several years wasted by not learning from your experiences. By asking yourself these questions, you'll learn much more from your experiences and advance much farther and faster.

10.3 Lead with Initiative

> *"A good plan executed right now is better than a perfect plan executed next week."*
> — *General George S. Patton*

I've found a simple approach to handling resistance that has made a big difference in my career and my productivity. When I run into opposition from the comfortable status quo, I remind myself: "Force the issue!" Problematic situations don't resolve themselves. They don't get better with time, they fester. The sooner we dive into problems with action, the sooner they are resolved. This often helps to minimize the overall damage done.

When it's clear what should be done, take that first step. The path may become clearer as you take one step at a time. For example, when I receive new information about a project and it's disappointing news that may derail my goals, instead of sitting on it and dreading the outcome, I summarize the situation and share it with the appropriate people so we may be able to do something about it. Even involving others in the thinking process helps to move it along. The key is to create action that moves the problem toward a resolution.

I used to brood over what I should do about a given situation. Now, I feel more comfortable after I've put things in motion and committed to "controlling what I can control." This means taking on an ownership mentality rather than a victim mentality. Instead of complaining, I'll ask, "What can I do to improve the situation?" Then I get busy taking action. Even if there is a horrible outcome that may be lingering, the sheer activity of doing what I can to minimize it provides relief and takes my mind off dwelling on more negative aspects. Since whatever you focus on grows, when you focus on the action you're taking to minimize the problem, the problem will continue to shrink.

In the popular Broadway show *Hamilton*, there is a song titled "The Room Where It Happens" during a scene in which Alexander Hamilton, Thomas Jefferson, and James Madison convene to negotiate the location of our nation's capital in exchange for approval of the nation's financial plan. I love that song. What it represents to me is that those in the room have the ability to influence events and outcomes that stretch far beyond that room. It's an honor to be in that room.

Again, recall that with great power comes great responsibility. You are in the room for a reason. You have a seat at the table for a reason. Speak your ideas. If you see problems, share those too. It's better for others to hear your dissenting voice early, when they can do something about it, rather than during a postmortem when all of you are lamenting a poor outcome.

10.4 Get in the Game

I was recently recognized — along with a number of people from my project team — for a Merit Award from my company. This is an honor. My boss told me one of the key differences he saw between teams making things happen and those that didn't was a "willingness to get in the game." He explained, "There are many sitting along the sidelines of life. They are afraid or don't want to get their hands dirty doing the hard but necessary work." Choose to get in the game.

As Dolly Parton said, "If your actions inspire others to dream more, learn more, do more, and become more, you are a leader." Choose to be a leader. There are fewer who choose this difficult path, but the rewards are so much greater. The first duty of a leader is optimism. You must have a vision and be committed. As former president of Notre Dame Father Theodore Hesburgh said, "You can't blow an uncertain trumpet." Be resolute, and be willing to get in the game.

10.5 Learn from Seth Godin on Being Unique

In March 2016, I was fortunate to attend "An Evening with Seth Godin" put on by the Harrisburg Regional Chamber of Commerce. Over five hundred people packed the Hershey Lodge & Convention Center to hear Godin speak. He didn't disappoint.

Seth Godin, author of eighteen books, is considered one of today's most influential business thinkers. I read one of Godin's books, *Linchpin*, and found it enlightening as to how organizations and individuals are evolving to bring their "art" and unique gifts to the marketplace. Below were my three key takeaways from the event:

1) The New Normal: Customers Want Customization

In the early 1900s, Henry Ford ushered in the Industrial Age. At first, it was all about standardization ("You can have your car any color you want as long as it's black.") and making things faster and cheaper in mass quantities. This worked for a while. Mass production led to mass marketing, mass sales, and the growth of companies like Ford's skyrocketed.

In the Internet Age, customers are now seeking customization for their specific needs. Companies and customers are happiest when they're as unique and self-determining as possible. We can perform Google searches and find the solutions to our very particular desires with a few keystrokes. We want customization, and we can receive it. In today's world, organizations that offer customized and added value products and services are the ones that thrive.

2) The Connected World: We Create Value Together

With such access to an abundance of information, below are six abilities that have become increasingly more valuable:

i) **Coordination:** Great things aren't accomplished alone. There is value in bringing people together. Get the right people to show up for a meeting, event, or conference.

ii) **Trust:** Everything we say and do is either building or eroding trust. Are we consistent in living up to our commitment to our customers? Trust is critical.

iii) **Attention:** In an information-overload age, will people willingly give you their most valuable resource — attention? Create content that continues to merit attention.

iv) **Exchange of Ideas:** Match people with problems with those who have insight to solve all or a portion of the problem.

v) **Generosity:** Abundantly share ideas. Give without demand of repayment. Abundance will flow back.

vi) **Art:** We are all unique human beings with different skills, abilities, education, and backgrounds. We are more valuable when contributing more of who we are and sticking out rather than shying away to conform in a machine-like manner.

3) Purple Cows: Be Remarkable

Godin reminded the audience that standing out is a strength: "Cows are boring. Nobody talks about a cow. But a Purple Cow? That would be worth talking about." Godin makes the point that marketing is no longer slapping a brand on a product or service to attract attention. The product or service itself has to be so remarkable that it's *worth* talking about.

The question is, what is your superpower — the unique value you bring to the marketplace? This could be your connections, creativity, leadership, technical knowledge, or ability. Organizations that are remarkable will thrive. These are the ones comprised of individuals bringing their art into the workplace to support the organization's mission.

10.6 Care Personally and Challenge Directly

> *"The best executive is one who has sense enough to pick*
> *good people to do what he wants done, and the self-*
> *restraint enough to keep from meddling with them while*
> *they do it."*
> — *Theodore Roosevelt*

As a leader, it's important for you to be more concerned with the welfare of others than with how they think about you. This is a difficult trait to adopt. As Kim Scott discusses in her book *Radical Candor*, it's important to lead with both head *and* heart. Leaders need to be willing to enter into courageous conversations. This is done by caring personally and challenging directly.

By loving the people you lead, you can venture forth into the messiness of caring and challenging. Know the people you lead. Know who they are as people, what their backgrounds are, their family situations, and what is important to them. This will help you to know when to be firm and when to be flexible.

10.7 Enter into Uncomfortable Conversations

> *"A person's success in life can usually be measured by the*
> *number of uncomfortable conversations he or she is*
> *willing to have."*
> — *Tim Ferriss*

At a political event I attended, Connecticut Governor Dan Malloy stood up and addressed the crowd. One phrase stuck with me: "It is difficult to tell people hard truths. They'd rather be lied to."

In the short term, we all want to be lied to about everything being great, regardless of whether we've put in the necessary work and effort to achieve that greatness. But in the long term, if we truly aspire toward excellence or a better life we need to be open to the truth, not just the things that are easy to hear. We need to be open to receiving *and* delivering these hard truths.

How do you become this leader? You do this by setting clear expectations and then holding yourself and others accountable. One way to communicate your expectations is to put it in writing to remove ambiguity. Allow others an opportunity to raise questions. Explain the "why" behind a decision or course of action. Lay out the consequences of violating expectations up-front.

10.8 Teach Others to Fish

it's tempting and often faster to complete a task yourself rather than to do it through and with others. But this is a shortsighted and unsustainable tactic because others will continually be dependent upon you. Therefore, remember the proverb "Give a man a fish and you feed him for a day. Teach a man to fish and you feed him for a lifetime."

Life is not a race. We all move at different paces. Never discourage anyone who continually makes progress, no matter how slow.

Former U.K. prime minister Benjamin Disraeli said, "The greatest good you can do for another is not just to share your riches, but to reveal to him his own." This is leadership — the practice of pulling more out of a person than they thought possible.

10.9 Transform from Lone Nut into Leader
Find Your First Follower

Michael Jordan's famed career would have never reached the level it did without his first follower, Scottie Pippen. *The first follower is what transforms a lone nut into a leader.*

Courageously Follow and Show Others

Early in in his career, Jordan scored points at an incredible rate, but he was a "lone nut" with his work ethic. After Pippen joined the Bulls, he and Jordan would play one-on-one to boost their individual skills.

Pippen followed Jordan's lead regarding work ethic and learned skills from him. It worked. This level of commitment rubbed off on the rest of the team and ultimately carried the Chicago Bulls to six NBA Championships. *The best way to make a movement is to courageously follow and show others how to follow.*

If you're looking to create a movement within your office, area, or company, who would be your Scottie Pippen? Who would be the person who will take your vision and match your intensity? Alternatively, will you have the courage and/or humility to be Scottie Pippen in service of someone else's vision to help start a movement and create greatness?

Care for Your Followers

Shortly after taking on a leadership role, my wife and I had dinner with a family friend of ours. As we were talking, I shared my new role and how I was both excited and nervous in taking on the new role with direct reports. She responded, "You'll do better than most just because you care." That stuck with me and I tried to live up to it.

10.10 Overcome Resistance to Change

Of course, we naturally resist change. You, me, and everyone around us has some natural aversion toward change. President Woodrow Wilson was only partially jesting when he said, "If you want to make enemies, try to change something."

As a leader, it's important to listen to those around you. When the facts merit it, you need to be able to change your mind. One of the dangers we can fall victim to — especially when we have found some success — is to become comfortable and fixed in our current situation and way of thinking. Founder of the American Red Cross Clara Barton voiced her opinion: "It irritates me to be told how things have always been done. ... I defy the tyranny of precedent. I cannot afford the luxury of a closed mind."

In the movie *Glory*, Colonel Shaw, played by Matthew Broderick, reluctantly takes on the role as leader of one of the first black regiments in the Union army fighting the Confederates. Realizing he needs help, he promotes Morgan Freeman's character to become the first black sergeant who himself wasn't seeking to be a leader. He says, "Thank you, Colonel, but I'm not so sure I wanted this." Colonel Shaw replies, "I know how you feel." Leadership comes to those who seek it as well as those who are promoted out of necessity and must rise up to play the hand they've been dealt.

★ ★ ★

Start by leading yourself first. By leading with your example, you'll gain the respect of those around you. As you adopt followers, you will be in a position to move mountains!

Take Action

- ☐ Use a journal to record the important events of your life, your goals, your struggles, and your accomplishments.
- ☐ Take note of books you may want to read and places you'd like to visit.
- ☐ Consciously select a person whom you wish to emulate and become their follower. Engage them and ask them questions about how they've done what they've done.
- ☐ Be generous with your knowledge, and lead others by teaching them what you know.
- ☐ Listen to your calling and lead courageously by listening to your gut.

Read These Books:

- ☐ *Ego Is the Enemy* by Ryan Holiday
- ☐ *The Autobiography of Benjamin Franklin* by Benjamin Franklin
- ☐ *Lead Yourself First* by Raymond M. Kethledge and Michael S. Erwin

CONCLUDING THOUGHT

During my spiritual reading this morning, I was posed the question, "If you died today, what would you wish you had done differently?" Another way of phrasing that question is, "What is it that you wish to do before you die?" In many ways, this book is the answer to that question for me. We will all die. That's a natural part of life. One of the most important things for me to do during my time on Earth is to share the wisdom and experiences I have gained during my lifetime so that the path may be easier for those who follow me.

Wisdom, like Love, is most valuable when it's shared.

This book was written with the intention of sharing my wisdom and my experiences with my children and any readers who open it. The thought that I've been able to pass along these ideas brings me peace. During the next phase of my life, I'll continue to look for ways of improving life for myself and those around me, and search for ways to share so others may benefit. I am thrilled you've stayed with me this long and hope it has been of value to you.

If you are so inclined, I would love to hear from you about how this book may have impacted your life or a loved one you gave it to.

Dads — if you have any wisdom that you yourself would like to pass along to others, I welcome your input!

Feel free to reach out to me with any questions you may have. Who knows, maybe hearing from you and addressing your questions will help us make the world a better place by spreading Dad's Wisdom.

God bless you on your own journey.

READING LIST

Not all readers are leaders, but all leaders are readers. Leaders at their core must be open to new ideas and continually growing or else risk being left behind. In order to offer better service, learning and growth of new methods is also helpful. This is a list of recommended books by chapter.

Chapter 1: Start with Your Desire
- *Think and Grow Rich* by Napoleon Hill
- *The Magic of Thinking Big* by David J. Schwartz
- *The Instant Millionaire* by Mark Fisher
- *The Alchemist* by Paulo Coelho
- *The Power of Intention* by Dr. Wayne W. Dyer
- *Rich Dad, Poor Dad* by Robert T. Kiyosaki

Chapter 2: Clarify Your Goal
- *The ONE Thing* by Gary W. Keller and Jay Papasan
- *Goals!* by Brian Tracy
- *See You at the Top* by Zig Ziglar
- *Unlimited Power* by Tony Robbins
- *The Millionaire Real Estate Investor* by Gary Keller

Chapter 3: Adjust Your Attitude
- *Who Moved My Cheese?* by Spencer Johnson
- *The Power of Positive Thinking* by Norman Vincent Peale
- *Success Through a Positive Mental Attitude* by Napoleon Hill and W. Clement Stone
- *No Excuses!* by Brian Tracy

- *The Power of Focus* by Jack Canfield, Mark Victor Hansen, and Les Hewitt
- *First Things First* by Stephen R. Covey
- *Over the Top* by Zig Ziglar
- *The Five Major Pieces to the Life Puzzle* by Jim Rohn
- *Outliers* by Malcolm Gladwell

Chapter 4: Value Your Time

- *The 7 Habits of Highly Effective People* by Stephen R. Covey
- *Eat that Frog!* by Brian Tracy
- *Getting Things Done* by David Allen
- *The 80/20 Principle* by Richard Koch

Chapter 5: Manage Your Finances

- *The Richest Man in Babylon* by George S. Clason
- *ChooseFI: Your Blueprint to Financial Independence* by Chris Mamula, Brad Barrett, and Jonathan Mendonsa
- *The Millionaire Next Door* by Thomas J. Stanley and William D. Danko
- *The Simple Path to Wealth* by J.L. Collins
- *Common Sense on Mutual Funds* by John C. Bogle
- *Your Money or Your Life* by Vicki Robin and Joe Dominguez
- *Personal Finance for Dummies* by Eric Tyson
- *Transforming Debt into Wealth* by John Cummuta
- *The Total Money Makeover* by Dave Ramsey
- *Money* by Tony Robbins
- *How to Invest in Real Estate* by Joshua Dorkin and Brandon Turner

Chapter 6: Sell Your Ideas

- *The Go-Giver* by Bob Burg and John David Mann
- *The Speed of Trust* by Stephen M.R. Covey
- *SPIN Selling* by Neil Rackham

- *The NEW Conceptual Selling* by Robert B. Miller and Stephen E. Heiman
- *The Greatest Salesman in the World* by Og Mandino
- *Tell to Win* by Peter Guber
- *Speak to Win* by Brian Tracy
- *Getting to Yes* by Robert Fisher and William Ury
- *How I Raised Myself from Failure to Success in Selling* by Frank Bettger
- *High Probability Selling* by Jacques Werth and Nicholas E. Ruben
- *The Challenger Sale* by Matthew Dixon and Brent Adamson

Chapter 7: Think Through Your Decisions

- *As a Man Thinketh* by James Allen
- *Thinking for a Change* by John C. Maxwell
- *Principles* by Ray Dalio
- *The Three Signs of a Miserable Job* by Patrick Lencioni
- *A 2nd Helping of Chicken Soup for the Soul* by Jack Canfield and Mark Victor Hansen
- *Blink* by Malcolm Gladwell
- *Nudge* by Richard H Thaler and Cass R. Sunstein
- *Profiles in Courage* by John F. Kennedy
- *Good to Great* by Jim Collins

Chapter 8: Connect with Your Family and Friends

- *How to Win Friends and Influence People* by Dale Carnegie
- *The 5 Love Languages* by Gary Chapman
- *The 7 Habits of Highly Effective Families* by Stephen R. Covey
- *Men Are from Mars, Women Are from Venus* by John Gray
- *Raising Positive Kids in a Negative World* by Zig Ziglar
- *Courtship After Marriage* by Zig Ziglar
- *I'm Proud of You* by Tim Madigan
- *Boundaries* by Dr. Henry Cloud and Dr. John Townsend

- *The Art of Empathy* by Karla McLaren
- *Tribe of Millionaires* by David Osborn, Pat Hiban, Mike McCarthy, and Tim Rhode

Chapter 9: Foster Your Faith

- The Bible (start with the Gospels and the Acts of the Apostles, then Proverbs and Wisdom)
- *The Biggest Lie in the History of Christianity* by Matthew Kelly
- *Believe It: My Journey of Success, Failure, and Overcoming the Odds* by Nick Foles
- *Resisting Happiness* by Matthew Kelly
- *Magnificent Obsession* by Lloyd C. Douglas
- *Success Is Never Ending, Failure Is Never Final* by Robert H. Schuller
- *The Robe* by Lloyd C. Douglas
- *The Shack* by Wm. Paul Young
- *Jesus and the Jewish Roots of Mary* by Brant Pitre
- *Rediscover Jesus* by Matthew Kellly

Chapter 10: Lead by Your Example

- *The Autobiography of Benjamin Franklin* by Benjamin Franklin
- *Lead Yourself First* by Raymond M. Kethledge and Michael S. Erwin
- *Linchpin* by Seth Godin
- *Leaders Ought to Know* by Phillip Van Hooser
- *The Freak Factor* by David Rendall
- *The Law of Success* by Napoleon Hill
- *Atomic Habits* by James Clear
- *Ego Is the Enemy* by Ryan Holiday
- *Team of Rivals: The Political Genius of Abraham Lincoln* by Doris Kearns Goodwin
- *Titan: The Life of John D. Rockefeller, Sr.* by Ron Chernow
- *The Last Lecture* by Randy Pausch

ACKNOWLEDGMENTS

Writing this book has been an incredible journey and process for me. There are so many people that have come into my life who don't know what a profound impact they have had on me. While there will always be more to thank, below are ones who have helped with significant experiences spanning both my personal and professional life.

Mom & Dad: You were my first role models. Thank you for your loving guidance and example.

Mom & Dad R.: Thank you for raising Dana with love.

Rebecca & Ben, Karen & Jordan, David & Nicole, Katie & Luke: I'm grateful that you're in my life. Thanks for road trips, board games, and general silliness growing up and efforts to stay engaged despite the miles between us.

Marla: Thank you for the thoughtful books you gave to me over the years.

Greg, Bill, Dan, Andre, & Bob: I learned sales, 401(k) investing, and perseverance under your tutelage. Thanks for your instruction and patience.

Chuck: Thanks for taking a chance on me for a new venture and providing coaching.

Justin & Jeff: It was a fun ride. I'm glad we got to launch it together.

Gary: Your technical expertise is exceeded only by your heart as a teacher.

Todd: Thoughts *really are* Things. Thanks for helping me get the right mental attitude.

Tommy: Grateful for your friendship, leadership coaching, and belief in me.

Warren: Thanks for the leadership opportunity and your continued example.

James: I appreciate the ever-growing trust you gave me and confidence you instilled.

Phillip: You've been a life-changer! Keep going 140 mph and living at the Red Line.

Jason: You're an awesome partner! There's a reason you're consistently the best.

Tim: I enjoyed our conversations twenty years ago and enjoy them even more now.

Bill: From bookstore basketball to leading our dorm — thanks for the teaming.

John: Your advice on speaking up in a meeting made a bigger impact that you can imagine.

Tony, Mahesh, Dan, Jerry, Andrew, & Jeff: Development of our team approach to win a project together was an experience I'll always be grateful for.

Mark, Chuck, John, Dave, Mary, Brian, George, Hal, Glenn, Mitesh, Dan, John, Karen, Craig, Jonathan, & Dave: Thank you for assembling top talented professionals and creating a vibrant environment with everyone committed to going all-out to make things happen. I feel privileged to work alongside you.

John: From client to confidant, your friendship was a turning point in my life.

Tucker, Guillermo, & Chad: Thanks for starting an incredible journey.

Chuck, Kelly, Neil, Rich, Tim, Steve, Charlie, Joe, Josh, Steve, Beth, Shawn, & John: Amazing what a transparent and committed partnership can create. Excited to continue in the spirit of *The Go-Giver* to find ways to give more and serve more people together.

Quad, Ryan, Huggins, Dave, Toshi, Tommy, & Colleen: Memories created both on and off campus will be cherished forever. GO IRISH!

Vijay, Ryan, Michael, Nicole & Nikki: Your friendships have been there for the full gamut of emotions from laughs to tears.

John, Jerry & Tony: Thanks for sharing your personal leadership journeys with my newly formed sales management team and your ongoing examples.

Jay, Becky, Melissa, Jim, Dave, Chris, Beth, Robert, Tina, Haley, Billy, Chuck, & Jeff: Together we created durable, profitable growth while training the sales team to elevate to a whole new level. I enjoyed getting to know you individually and helping you grow.

Jim, Trish, Sean, Adel, Anthony, Rich, Ed, & Steve: Thank you for your solid faith and friendship.

Mark, Scott, & Kevin: Thanks for making work fun.

Jerry & The Legends: Career coaching was super helpful. Softball was most fun and memorable!

Bruce & The Big 4: Thanks for the running advice, laughter, and making the miles fun.

Concretely Speaking Toastmasters: I'm so grateful for all the public speaking support! Those were formative years.

Each of you poured out who you were and we all got better for it.

John David Mann, Bob Burg, Brian Tracy, Phillip Van Hooser, & Matt Faircloth: You inspire millions with your books. Please continue. I'm honored to have a contribution next to yours.

Jace Mattison & Clark Sheffield: Keep sharing stories on your *Millionaires Unveiled* podcast.

Jonathan Mendosa & Brad Barrett: Your *ChooseFI* podcast is bringing hope to a community.

Thanks to the book production team: Grace Kerina, Josh Raab, Cathy Suter, Andrew Bell, and Amélie Cherlin.

Dana: I knew you were a good match for me when you used a coupon for our first dinner out! Your natural frugality, patience, and support have enabled me to meet many of my financial and career goals. Thank you for providing stability for me and the kids and for giving me space to dream. Thank you for reminding me what true treasure is.

DAD'S LITTLE INDEX OF WISDOM

ABOUT THE AUTHOR

Mark Fennell is an author, speaker, and business professional with twenty-two years of experience in sales and sales management. After almost being fired three times for poor sales performance, he decided to focus on honing and utilizing his unique strengths. This eventually led to recognition for Top 3 in sales performance in his division of a global Fortune 500 company, accumulating wealth in the top 10 percent of the country, and generating income in the top 1 percent of individuals in the United States.

Mark enjoys reading, running, and spending time with his family. He has read over four hundred books, amassed a collection of over five hundred quotes, and run five marathons including the Boston Marathon.

Mark and his wife, Dana, have been married for eighteen years and reside in a suburb of Philadelphia. They are blessed with three children.

Made in the USA
Middletown, DE
16 September 2023

38538974R00132